Greenfield Village
and
the Henry Ford Museum

Greenfield Village
and
the Henry Ford Museum

by

The Henry Ford Museum Staff

Crown Publishers, Inc.   **New York**

Contents

Greenfield Village and Henry Ford Museum: "Americana Preserved"

Preface by Dr. Donald A. Shelley, President

Greenfield Village, founded by Henry Ford in 1929 as a tribute to the creative genius and achievements of Thomas Alva Edison, is more than that. It is a tribute to the genius and achievements of innumerable Americans whose hard work, endurance, and ideals moved this nation from thirteen loosely connected colonies through the Industrial Revolution of the nineteenth century and into the Space Age.

The fascinating story of that transition, told not with just words but with original buildings, priceless

Henry Ford testing his Quadricycle on the morning of June 4, 1896, painted by Irving R. Bacon.

objects, association items, early photographs, and rare documents, crams the following pages. These are not empty symbols or one individual's concepts, but genuine, real, living history, for in them and through them Greenfield Village is truly "where American history comes to life . . ."

Today, perhaps even more than when Mr. Ford began to preserve Americana fifty years ago, "we ought to know more about them [the men who founded our country] and how they lived, and the force and courage they had."

And starting from his original premise that "a piece of machinery, or anything that is made is like a book, if you can read it," Greenfield Village and Henry Ford Museum continue to search out, acquire, preserve,

Assembling a complete set of McGuffey Readers was the first collecting effort of Henry and Clara Ford.

exhibit, and publish information on every aspect of our culture and civilization. We are still collecting "the history of our people as written into things their hands made and used," with emphasis upon the *original* item, the *full-size* item (not the model), the *manufactured* item (not the prototype), and especially the *key* item telling the story of actual development. We are in fact a general museum of American history established for educational purposes, and we focus on our goals and achievements under the free enterprise system. We are the visualization, the embodiment, of the American dream.

Greenfield Village presents a broad panorama of life in America beginning with the early settlers' cabins, moving forward through the small-town main street to the village green, and thence to the relatively modest birthplaces of some of our most famous Americans. We see the first establishment of home industries, the eighteenth- and nineteenth-century wooden craft shops, and the later nineteenth-century brick factories of the Industrial Revolution. Preserved also are many picturesque smaller buildings and appurtenances of our bygone days for future students to study and enjoy. And bringing ancient crafts to life again, as well as reviving early modes of transportation and commerce, can lead only to *greater understanding* and *appreciation* of the American way of life.

Henry Ford Museum, by contrast, provides in three-dimensional form more of the specifics and sharpens the focus upon that way of life by presenting in chronological sequence the artifacts, tools, and machinery used by it. The Decorative Arts Galleries with their numerous period settings, the Street of twenty-two early American Shops, and the Mechanical Arts Hall—covering agriculture, home arts, industrial machinery, steam and electric power, lighting, communication, and transportation in all its forms—provide the broadest and most comprehensive assemblage of true Americana to be found anywhere in the world. Unlike the Village collections, here one can explore at close range and in greater depth the step-by-step development of any form of Americana that interests him. And as he makes his way across the Museum to his chosen field, he is exposed to related areas, thereby inevitably enlarging his field of interest.

For the really "gone" collector who requires further assistance in the form of research, there is a corps of dedicated curators, endless study collections, an excellent Museum research library, and the incomparable Ford Archives containing over fourteen million documents, manuscripts, books, and priceless photographs. A never-ending sequence of special exhibitions, seminars or forums, and several annual lecture series assist further in bringing the Museum collection to life. An active publications program also disseminates knowledge of American history in general, and of the Museum collections in particular, not only to the members and "Friends" of the Museum, but to the million and a half visitors from this country and abroad who pass through our Village every year.

Perhaps the most significant aspect of this new volume, then, is that here for the first time it is possible to survey broadly the contents of Greenfield Village and Henry Ford Museum in all their diversity. Every American (no matter where his place of birth, his profession, his interests) and every member of his family (no matter what his age, sex, or hobby) will find something here to broaden his understanding and give him new pride in his priceless American heritage.

Clara and Henry Ford at home.

Greenfield Village

**Introduction by
Robert G. Wheeler,
Vice-President,
Research and Interpretation**

At 10:00 A.M. on rainy October 21, 1929, a locomotive of Civil War vintage pulled a baggage car and two mustard-colored coaches up to Smiths Creek Station in Greenfield Village. At this brick depot Thomas Alva Edison had been ejected sixty-seven years earlier by an irate conductor for spilling phosphorus on the floor of his train and setting it on fire.

Aboard this special train were Mr. Edison, President Herbert Hoover, and Mr. and Mrs. Henry Ford, who had come together in Dearborn to dedicate the Village and the Henry Ford Museum. Among the as-

President Herbert Hoover and the aging inventor, Thomas Alva Edison, arriving at Smiths Creek Station where they joined Henry Ford (far left) and numerous world dignitaries for the dedication of Greenfield Village and the Henry Ford Museum.

sembled guests at the dedication ceremonies were such world notables as Orville Wright, Madame Curie, John D. Rockefeller, Jr., Will Rogers, Owen D. Young, and Charles M. Schwab. They were driven on the muddy Village streets in horse-drawn closed carriages to inspect construction progress.

Greenfield Village, a preserved American village scene, today occupies a good part of the 260 acres set aside by Henry Ford to house the more than one hundred structures moved here from original sites across the nation. Together, these buildings preserve the physical surroundings of a typical American community whose roots date to the seventeenth century and illustrate the marriage of home life, manufacturing, and transportation in the development of this nation.

The Village falls naturally into certain specific areas of interest and activity: (1) the humble homes and the workshops of American industrial giants whose inventive genius shaped the world we know today; (2) the earlier houses of our ancestors and a continuing demonstration of their home life from the 1640s to the late nineteenth century; (3) the village green—hub of community activities—with its church, inn, town hall, school, offices, shops, courthouse, and the other buildings essential to daily living patterns; (4) the industrialization of America, proceeding from the home workshops of individual craftsmen to the rapidly growing factory system of the Industrial Revolution.

Here, in one great outdoor museum, is the story of American life covering three and one-half centuries. Here is the feel, the look, the tangible evidence of how Americans built and decorated their houses, conducted their affairs, educated their young. Here is evidenced the social revolution as America moved from the home crafts to an industrial nation. Here American history comes to *detailed* life as craftsmen work at daily tasks; and special events such as the annual Country Fair, the Rug Hooking Bee, the Muzzle Loaders Festival, and the Old Car Festival re-create aspects of bygone days.

Henry Ford carefully defined his goals for Greenfield Village. "When we are through, we shall have reproduced American life as lived; and that, I think, is the best way of preserving at least a part of our history and tradition. For by looking at things people used and that show the way they lived, a better and truer impression can be gained than could be had in a month of reading—even if there were books whose author had the facilities to discover the minute details of the older life."

These goals, as this book will show, are being achieved.

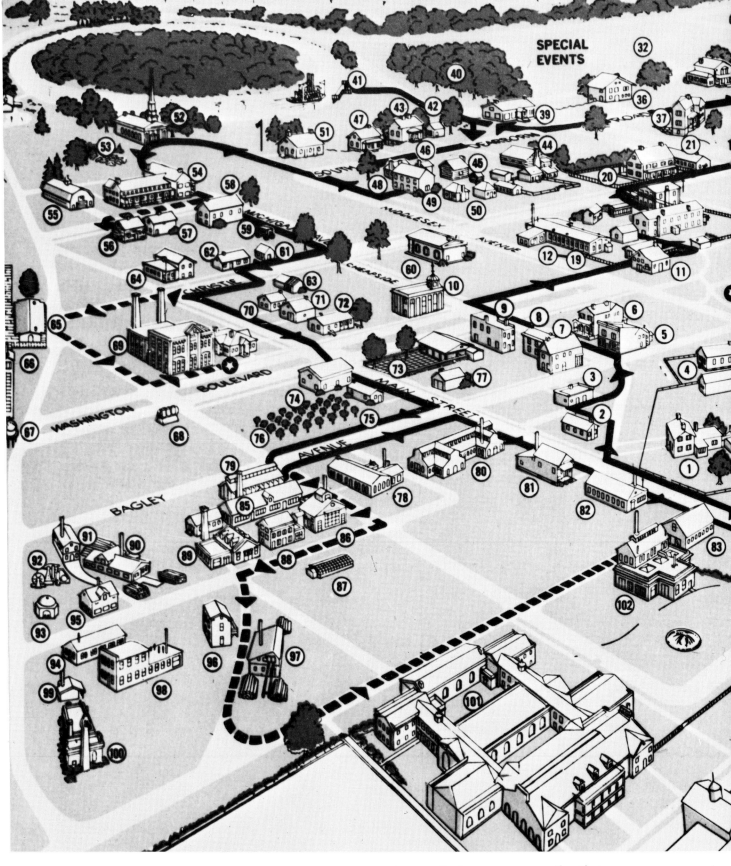

MAP OF GREENFIELD VILLAGE

SPECIAL EVENTS

MAP LEGEND

1. Henry Ford Birthplace
2. Edsel Ford Workshop
3. 58 Bagley Avenue Shop
4. Miller School
5. Wright Cycle Shop
6. Wright Birthplace
7. Magill Jewelry Store
8. Heinz House
9. Grimm Jewelry Store
10. Sir John Bennett
    Jewelry Shop
11. Edison West Orange
    Laboratory
12-19. Edison Menlo
    Park Compound
12. Carbon Shed
13. Electric Train
14. Carpenter Shed
15. Machine Shop
16. Glass House
17. Edison's Laboratory
18. Laboratory Dump
19. Office and Library
20. Sarah Jordan Boarding
    House
21. Fort Myers Laboratory
22. Whittier Tollhouse-
    Shoe Shop
23. Ackley Covered Bridge
24. Susquehanna House
25. Plympton House
26. Cape Cod Windmill
27. Cotswold Forge
28. Cotswold Dovecote
29. Cotswold Stable
30. Cotswold "Rose Cottage"
31. Secretary Pearson House

46. Mattox House
47. John Chapman House
48. George Washington Carver Memorial
49. Abe Lincoln Courthouse
50. Slave Quarters
51. Scotch Settlement School
52. Martha-Mary Chapel
53. Garden of the Leavened Heart
54. Clinton Inn
55. Addison Ford Barn
56. Pioneer Log Cabin
57. Richard Gardner House
58. Waterford General Store
59. "Owl" Night-Lunch Wagon
60. The Town Hall
61. Dr. Howard's Office
62. Phoenixville Post Office
63. Tintype Studio
64. Plymouth House
65. Smiths Creek Depot
66. Steam-Powered Sawmill
67. Railroad Water Tower
68. Electric Generating Unit
69. Edison Illuminating Company

Gatehouse to Greenfield Village.

70. Currier Shoe Shop
71. Kingston Cooper Shop
72. Village Blacksmith Shop
73. Village Lunch Stand
74. Plymouth Carding Mill
75. Hanks Silk Mill
76. Mulberry Grove
77. Deluge Fire House
78. Lapeer Machine Shop
79. Sandwich Glass Plant
80. Armington & Sims Machine Shop
81. Loranger Gristmill
82. Village Print Shop
83. William Ford Barn
84. Detroit Floral Clock
85. Village Planing Mill
86. Harahan Sugar Mill
87. Village Greenhouse
88. Cotton Gin Mill
89. Fairfield Rice Mill
90. Stony Creek Sawmill
91. Spofford Up-and-Down Sawmill
92. Walking Beam Engine
93. Haycock Boiler
94. Village Boiler Shop
95. Martinsville Cider Mill
96. Richart Carriage Shop
97. Tripp Up-and-Down Sawmill
98. Mack Avenue Ford Plant
99. Macon Brick Works
100. Haggerty Power House
101. Education Building and Lovett Hall
102. Soybean Laboratory
103. Henry Ford Museum

VILLAGE ROAD

VILLAGE ENTRANCE

HENRY FORD MUSEUM

32. Special Events Field
33. Noah Webster House
34. Edison Homestead
35. Ann Arbor House
36. Watchmaker's Chalet
37. Luther Burbank Birthplace
38. Burbank Garden Office
39. Stephen Foster Birthplace
40. Village Picnic Grove
41. Edison Steamboat "Suwanee"
42. Charles Steinmetz Cabin
43. George Matthew Adams Birthplace
44. McGuffey School
45. McGuffey Birthplace

13

I. Captains of Industry

As the nineteenth century moved toward its close, four giant figures, whose inventive genius would change the habits of the world, were becoming known. All, well known to one another, were to be associated during their lifetimes through friendship, and through the preservation of their family homes and their workshops in Greenfield Village.

Thomas Alva Edison (1847–1931) had already gained world renown through his incandescent electric lamp, his stock ticker, the phonograph, the electric pen or duplicator, the motion picture camera and projector. He had spent his ten most brilliant and creative years at Menlo Park, New Jersey, where he had established the world's first industrial research laboratory. During Edison's lifetime he was granted 1,093 patents, probably the greatest number ever issued to one man.

Orville (1867–1912) and Wilbur (1871–1948) Wright projected the world into the "air age" with the first power-driven, heavier-than-air machine which flew at Kitty Hawk, North Carolina, on December 17, 1903. Although Orville's first flight that day lasted only twelve seconds and covered one hundred and twenty feet, it catapulted civilization into the space era.

Henry Ford (1863–1947), a farm boy turned machinist, built his Quadricycle which he tested and drove in June, 1896. This vehicle inaugurated Ford's ambition to make a family car—a poor man's utility—which would replace the horse. It did this and much more, bringing about a social revolution affecting much of American life to the present day.

In 1919, Mr. Ford began the preservation of his own birthplace *(left),* a simple two-story clapboard midwestern farmhouse built in 1860 at Dearborn, Michigan, by his father William. He obtained every piece of original furniture and equipment that could be found; those that were unavailable he replaced with similar objects of the same period, such as the Victorian sofa and chairs in the parlor *(lower left).* His goal was to have the house look exactly as he remembered it from his childhood years. As a youth, he spent many hours at a workbench set up in a bedroom *(right)* where he devised a set of handmade tools and became, by the time he was fifteen, community watch repairman.

Interestingly enough, the last building Mr. Ford himself had moved to Greenfield Village, in 1944, was this same birthplace which he had meticulously restored on its original site twenty-five years earlier.

Mr. Ford never lost his interest in the land that had nurtured him. He fostered farming. He encouraged experimental gardening and wildlife conservation. He promoted aviation. He underwrote educational projects.

Orville and Wilbur Wright, the pioneer aviators, lived in the late nineteenth-century clapboard house *(below)* which was the family's home at Dayton, Ohio, for over forty years. The inventive brothers added numerous improvements to the home. They designed and constructed the spacious porch in 1892 and redesigned and installed the staircase, cherry banisters and posts leading to the second floor. Behind the house is a small white building, "the summer kitchen," which Mrs. Wright turned over to her active young sons for their printing and photographic activities.

The Wright brothers began their bicycle business in Dayton, Ohio, in 1892 when Orville was twenty-one and Wilbur twenty-five. The *Wright Cycle Shop (below)* consisted of a salesroom, office, storeroom, repair room, and machine shop. Money earned from the bicycle business financed the brothers' flying experiments. They built their early gliders and planes in this late Victorian remodeled brick building. Often referred to as the "Birthplace of Aviation," it was here that they constructed their first successful plane, the *Kitty Hawk (left)*. The room adjacent to the shop presently serves as a gallery for the display of early aviation photographs.

Orville Wright and his sister Katherine were born in the Dayton home, and grew up amid the unpretentious Victorian and turn-of-the-century furnishings displayed in the family parlor *(left)*. The mahogany flat-top desk with delicate floral inlay and brass rail at the top, a Victorian mahogany side chair with carved crest and horsehair slip-seat, and the upholstered rocking chair, one of three, are original to the house. The Wright kitchen *(below)*, like those in many midwestern homes, contained modern conveniences of the day including a gas cooking stove, gas lighting fixtures, and an "inside" water pump in the sink.

In the Wright machine shop *(below)* the equipment is kept in working order, a principle established by Mr. Ford early in his attempt to present a "living village." The Wrights' aviation experiments began with the air-pressure test bicycle *(right)* which, when pedaled rapidly, produced the effect of wind on the test vanes of the horizontal balance wheel. This device led to the Wrights' conception of the first wind tunnel used to obtain the data necessary for designing their airplanes. The shop is fitted with most of the original machinery.

Thomas Alva Edison, "Wizard of Menlo Park," founded the world's first industrial research center in the compound of buildings at Menlo Park, New Jersey. The laboratory, first building erected in the complex, was constructed in 1876 under the personal supervision of Mr. Edison's father. Its ground floor (near left) is shown illuminated by historic cardboard filament lamps. Edison worked in the compound from 1876 to 1886, the ten "golden years" considered to be his most inventive. He once told a close associate that it was his aspiration to produce within this complex one major invention every six months and one minor item every ten days. The inventor more than fulfilled his desire, for of the 1,093 patents achieved within his lifetime, 420 were the direct result of his labors at Menlo Park. On the evening of October 21, 1929, in celebration of the fiftieth anniversary of Thomas A. Edison's creation of the incandescent lamp, over three hundred world leaders, scientists, eminent citizens, and educators gathered together in Dearborn, Michigan, at a banquet attended by some of the most distinguished persons ever assembled at one time. After the banquet, the aging inventor, his former assistant Francis Jehl, President Hoover, and Mr. Ford adjourned to the Menlo Park Laboratory which, with the other Menlo Park buildings, had been carefully moved to Greenfield Village. At that time Edison's re-creation of his first lamp (left) not only marked the anniversary of that history-making event, but also commemorated the dedication of The Edison Institute, named in his honor. Mr. Ford considered the Menlo Park Compound his most important preservation effort.

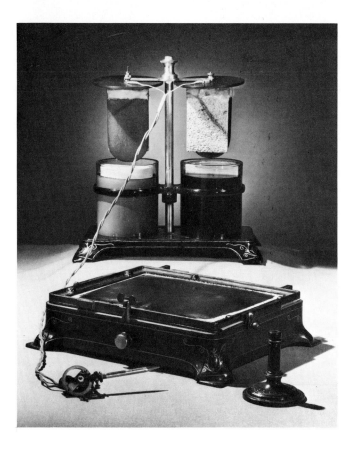

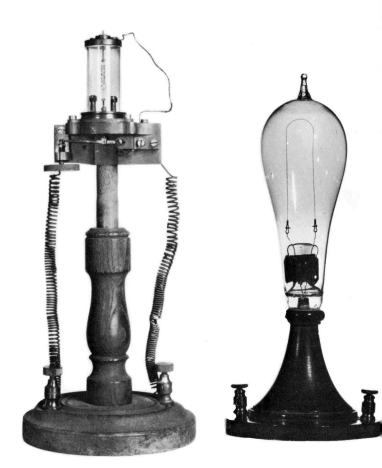

Although the most significant contribution that Edison and his staff made at Menlo Park was the development of a complete system of electrical engineering, it is often said that the greatest single invention was one which was never patented—the development of *organized technical research*. Each of Edison's research assistants was a specialist in his chosen field, directing individual "trial and error" efforts toward the development of practical inventions. From this concerted work came the electric pen *(above),* forerunner of modern stencil duplication; the incandescent lamps *(right);* the phonograph; the carbon telephone transmitter; and countless other inventions which affect our lives today. Housing the Edison business records was the handsome two-story brick office and library. The second floor *(below)* contains the comprehensive technical library used by his staff and administered by librarian Otto Moses. A cardboard filament street lamp stands in front of the Menlo Park Laboratory *(opposite).*

Several of Edison's employees lived at *Sarah Jordan's Boarding House* adjacent to the *Menlo Park Laboratory*. This residence was probably the first home in the world to be lighted by Edison's newly perfected lighting system. The electrified kerosene chandelier, attached to the exposed wiring, represents the first of many conveniences which the advent of practical electricity brought to the American home.

II. Bridge to the Past

In 1832 a covered bridge was built across Wheeling Creek between Washington and Greene Counties in southwestern Pennsylvania. It was named for Joshua Ackley, from whose land the great oak timbers for its construction were taken. Today, at Greenfield Village, this bridge leads one back in time to the residential area of private homes. Here is illustrated the progressive story of seventeenth-, eighteenth-, and nineteenth-century American architecture and home furnishings.

The earliest structure, the *Cotswold "Rose Cottage,"* is English. It stands on this American street as a reminder of those homes left behind by many immigrants to the New World. Nearby are the seventeenth-century contrasts: the simple one-room Massachusetts *Plympton House* and the expanded gentry-owned *Susquehanna House* from Maryland.

Chronologically, the next period represented is the eighteenth century by the New Hampshire *Secretary House.* Next door, in the nineteenth-century *Webster House* built at New Haven, Connecticut, in 1822, Noah Webster compiled his monumental work, *An American Dictionary of the English Language.*

Robert Frost, the great poet of rural New England, lived in the chaste Greek Revival *Ann Arbor House* while poet-in-residence at the University of Michigan. Across the street are the clapboard farmhouse from Ontario, Canada, built by Thomas A. Edison's grandfather, and the simple Massachusetts birthplace of Luther Burbank.

Close to the birthplace of Stephen Foster, removed to the Village from Lawrenceville, Pennsylvania, are the summer cabin used by the electrical wizard, Charles Steinmetz, near Schenectady, New York; the Pennsylvania log house in which William Holmes McGuffey was born; a memorial to George Washington Carver, a close friend of Henry Ford. Two simple nineteenth-century Michigan houses complete this area.

None of these famous American houses are mansions. None are built of brick or stone. All are modest in scale. All are scrupulously furnished to the period in which they were constructed. Each clearly represents the social scale on which the owner lived, and the region or area of his origins.

Here, along residential row, American history comes to life.

The English seventeenth-century limestone *Cotswold Cottage,* with its walled garden, barnyard, dovecote, and forge, recalls the Old World origins of many of New England's earliest settlers. This "Rose Cottage" was built in the early 1600s at Chedworth, Gloucestershire, in southwestern England, and was the home of a family of sheepherders. The English Tudor and Jacobean furniture throughout the house is oak, blackened by the smoke from roaring fires in its massive stone fireplaces. Wooden trenchers, burl bowls, and a leather "blackjack" used as a water dipper or drinking vessel are displayed on the opened gateleg table. An English brass lantern clock, circa 1630, is a luxurious appointment in such a simple home. The sheep in Greenfield Village are descendants of the famed "Cotswold Lions" imported by Henry Ford from the Cotswold Hills.

The *Cotswold Forge (right and above)*, built about 1620 at Snowshill in south-western England, was operated by members of the Stanley family for almost three hundred years. Wrought iron household utensils and farm tools are made by Village craftsmen in this, the oldest working blacksmith shop in the United States.

In the seventeenth century, birds from dovecotes much like the one below provided relief from smoked and salted meats during the harsh winter months.

The seventeenth-century *Cape Cod Windmill (left)* from West Yarmouth, Massachusetts, is one of the earliest in America. Corn and other grains were ground in this "tower" mill. The interior has a winding stairway which extends upward three stories from the ground level to the revolving roof area. Mammoth sails measuring fifty-four feet across must be spread with canvas, like the sails of a ship, before grinding begins.

The oldest American house in Greenfield Village originally stood on the property of Thomas Plympton in South Sudbury, Massachusetts. Plympton, who arrived in America as an indentured servant, was one of the founders of the Puritan settlement of Sudbury Plan-

tation in 1638. This one-room home, with its simple sheathed walls, open raftered ceiling, and central summer beam, is typical of New England colonial architecture of the earliest period. The furnishings reflect the stark simplicity of home life during the late seventeenth century on the New England frontier. Here, as in occasional seventeenth-century homes, a free-standing fireplace was built within the room to provide heat on all four sides. An unusual feature of *Plympton House* is the convenient inside covered well (visible to the left of the ladder in the bottom photograph). Since hostile Indians and wild animals roamed the land, it was also a safety factor.

The gracious six-room *Susquehanna House* from tidewater Maryland was occupied shortly after 1650 by Christopher Rousby, tax collector for King Charles II. This one-and-one-half-story home, one room deep, is furnished chiefly with English pieces of the seventeenth and early eighteenth centuries. Unlike most Americans, the affluent Rousbys could afford imported furnishings. One of the oldest pieces in the house is a carved oak wainscot chair dated 1626. In the kitchen, a Village craftsman, using bayberries and beeswax, demonstrates the homely art of candlemaking. Each year leaf tobacco, one of Maryland's principal crops in the seventeenth and eighteenth centuries, is cultivated in a field adjoining the house.

Henry Ford's meticulous attention to detail and his great feeling for the integrity of Greenfield Village and Henry Ford Museum are clearly demonstrated in the preservation of *Susquehanna House*. When he moved it to the Village, he not only brought the attractive little dairy house, but also the carved tombstone and last remains of the two Rousby brothers who had been buried in the garden a hundred yards from the house. The semiformal garden of boxwood and myrtle, typical of the region and period, follows the pattern of the British Union Jack. Crushed oyster shells were used for the pathways.

The simplified Georgian *Secretary House* from Exeter, New Hampshire, was built in 1750 by John Giddings, a prosperous merchant and shipbuilder. After 1790, it became the home of New Hampshire's first Secretary of State, Joseph Pearson. An inventory, taken at the time of Pearson's death in 1823, made it possible to furnish the home as it had been during his lifetime. The "best parlor" *(above, left)* contains New England Chippendale furniture dating from about 1760 to 1790, including a walnut side chair that belonged to George Washington. The dining room *(above, right),* with sliding shutters, is furnished with Queen Anne pieces. In the red bed-chamber is a New Hampshire Queen Anne high chest of drawers which originally belonged to the family of Josiah Bartlett (1729–1795), a signer of the Declaration of Independence and the first Governor of New Hampshire (1793–1795). Of special interest is the folding press bed which provided additional sleeping facilities.

The Federal-style home of Noah Webster (1758–1843) from New Haven, Connecticut, was designed and built by David Hoadley in 1822. An elliptical louvred window and modillion cornice are typical of Hoadley's interpretation of the Classical Revival style. The Webster family watched the "progress of this building. . . . A glad one was the day we moved into more commodious quarters. . . . We sat on low chairs and sewed the parlor carpet ourselves." At Christmas the fluted Ionic columns on the classic entrance porch are decorated with evergreen roping (left, top). Sprigs of holly, Christmas wreaths, and a candle-laden tree are cheery accents to this handsome house during the holiday season. In the home are many Webster association pieces. The silhouette (above) is a detail of a double portrait of Mr. and Mrs. Webster by Samuel Metford. The oil portrait of Mrs. Webster (left), and a companion painting of Mr. Webster, descended in the family. The Websters were able and gracious hosts. Their musicales, charade parties, and "old-time frolics" were diversions much praised by their austere New England neighbors.

Noah Webster is noted for his many literary efforts. His most important contribution to American literature was *An American Dictionary of the English Language,* first published in 1828 in two volumes. A manuscript page and a first edition of the *Dictionary* in original boards are important parts of the vast collection of Webster-related material housed in the Henry Ford Museum Research Library. Also contained in the collection are many holograph letters and numerous first editions of other Webster publications including his *Blue-Backed Speller.* Webster followed a disciplined routine of writing daily until 4:00 P.M. at the secretary-desk in the upstairs study, his favorite working place *(above).* The bedrooms *(left)* are furnished with Empire-style pieces and country furniture. Hooked rugs, popular in New England in the nineteenth century, cover the floors. The dining room *(right, top),* with the mahogany Hepplewhite table set for dessert, is furnished with Federal pieces. The painting, *A View Near Anthony's Nose, Hudson Highlands, New York,* by Thomas Chambers (active 1832 to circa 1866), provides an additional dimension to the sparkling interior. Rebecca and Noah Webster were proud parents. In a letter to her daughter Eliza, Mrs. Webster wrote, "Papa longs to see you all. I heard someone conversing in the drawing room [parlor] the other day and found him standing before your portraits. . . . We often talk together . . . of our singular happiness in our sons-in-law and daughters and such a promising bunch of grandchildren." The portraits of Eliza Webster Jones and her husband Henry are part of the Greenfield Village collections and hang in the parlor above the Empire black horsehair sofa, one of Mrs. Webster's most treasured pieces of furniture *(right, bottom).*

Stephen Foster (1826-1864), the composer of some of America's most loved music, was born in a simple house *(far right, bottom)* which was built about 1815 in Pittsburgh, Pennsylvania. The house is furnished with several pieces of Foster furniture including a tall-case clock, a pair of candelabra with brass figures, a drop leaf table, a four-poster rope-spring bed, and a green velvet upholstered Hepplewhite barrel-back chair *(near right)*. The Museum's Research Library contains several original Foster manuscripts as well as his flute, flageolet, and guitar. Foster songs which are still favorites today include "Oh, Susanna," "Beautiful Dreamer," "Old Folks at Home," and "Old Dog Tray," written in tribute to his childhood companion, a handsome setter. Behind the Foster birthplace is a sleepy lagoon where swans are interrupted by the happy chatter of visitors enjoying a nostalgic ride on the steamboat *Suwanee.*

One of the finest examples of midwestern Greek Revival architecture is the six-room home built in 1830 at Ann Arbor, Michigan, for Thompson Sinclair, a local politician. *Ann Arbor House* is furnished with Classical Revival and Empire pieces of the second quarter of the nineteenth century, including a painted pine watchcase *(near left)* in form of an eagle, circa 1810. Robert Frost (1874–1963) served as "poet-in-residence" at the University of Michigan and lived in this sophisticated home where he wrote several of his best poems.

Another example of midwestern Greek Revival architecture is the *Plymouth House (right)*, built in 1845 at Plymouth, Michigan, for Christian Fisher. Fisher, a local cobbler, made and sold shoes from this dwelling. Today it is used as a setting for pieces from the Henry Ford Museum Reproduction Program which includes furniture, glass, pottery, pewter, and textiles.

Samuel Ogden Edison, grandfather of world-renowned Thomas Alva Edison, built his clapboard house *(above)* in 1816 at Vienna, Ontario, Canada. Edison's parents, Samuel and Nancy Elliott, were married in the Sunday parlor in 1828. Young Tom, shown in an original daguerreotype taken in 1851, spent many summers in this comfortable home. In maturity, he fondly recalled the large, simple, farm-type kitchen with its "Moss Rose" pattern china. As part of a special exhibition, "Christmas at Greenfield Village," a guide demonstrates the old-fashioned pastime of taffy-pulling *(left)*.

John Brainerd Chapman, Henry Ford's favorite teacher at the Scotch Settlement School, lived in the modest frame dwelling *(far right, top)* built in 1860 near the Ford family farm in Springwells Township. The home is furnished with many pieces that Chapman and his wife once used, and also contains an impressive collection of Victorian chairs manufactured by the Detroit Chair Factory at Detroit, Michigan. The winter view of Suwanee Lagoon *(right, bottom)* shows the *Chapman House (right)* and the *George Matthew Adams Birthplace (left)*. The Adams house was built in 1833 at Saline, Michigan. George Matthew Adams was a well-known newspaper writer; Henry Ford took great pleasure in his inspirational column, "Today's Talk." On several occasions, Adams visited Greenfield Village and stayed in his childhood home.

The Pioneer Log Cabin (left) was built in the 1820s near Ford Road in Greenfield Township, Michigan, by John Salter, a German hermit and philosopher. It is typical of most dwellings constructed during Michigan's territorial period and is furnished with simple furniture and utilitarian accessories.

William Holmes McGuffey (1800–1873) was born in a one-room frontier cabin *(below, right)* located in Washington County, Pennsylvania. McGuffey—a school-teacher, college professor, and Presbyterian minister—is best remembered as author of a group of textbooks, *The Eclectic Readers,* published for the first six elementary grades. Millions of Americans, including Henry and Clara Bryant Ford as well as Orville and Wilbur Wright, used the famous books during their childhood. Country-made furniture donated by members of the McGuffey family was used to furnish the *Birthplace* at Greenfield Village. The flax wheel before the old stone fireplace and the dasher churn in front of the pottery-laden corner cupboard were necessities in rural nineteenth-century America.

Richard Gardner, one of the original settlers of the Scotch Settlement in Greenfield Township, Michigan, together with his wife and their ten children, lived in the small house *(right)* which he built in 1832. This building is similar to the *Pioneer Log Cabin,* except that it has the additional refinement of clapboard siding.

The Mattox House (left), constructed during the pre-Civil War days on Cottenham Plantation near Ways, Georgia, was used by a plantation overseer. Most of the crude furnishings are original possessions of the Mattox family and the house appears much as it did during the days of slavery.

Luther Burbank (1849–1926), the world-renowned horticulturist, was born in a frame house which was built about 1800 at Lancaster, Massachusetts. Country painted and decorated furniture, American folk art, and hooked rugs from the nineteenth century were used to furnish this colorful seven-room home. Samuel Burbank made the pine cradle (above) for his infant son Luther. Burbank devoted his entire life to the study, development, and improvement of plant life. This distinguished pioneer plant innovator improved and produced more varieties of flowers, fruits, vegetables, trees, grains, and grasses than any other individual.

The Victorian-style office *(above)* once stood in a corner of Burbank's experimental gardens at Santa Rosa, California. From this frame building, he administered his nursery business. Burbank's oak rolltop desk, shown in the colorful portrait *(right)* by Irving R. Bacon, remains in the garden office.

Charles Steinmetz (1865–1923), the electrical wizard and mathematician, constructed a summer retreat *(left)* in 1896 on the banks of the Vielie Creek near Schenectady, New York. During his lifetime Steinmetz obtained over two hundred patents; he is credited with more than one hundred electrical inventions.

Numerous and varied herbs were used in the creation of the *Garden of the Leavened Heart (above)*. The garden, which follows a medieval design, illustrates Mrs. Henry Ford's keen interest in horticulture.

The Floral Clock (below), a beloved landmark in Detroit, was built in 1893 and operated by waterpower at the entrance to Waterworks Park. When relocated in Greenfield Village, it was converted to a weight and pendulum system. The face of this historic clock is made up of some ten thousand plants.

53

The *Addison-Ford Barn (above),* which had been erected about 1885 in northwestern Detroit, was moved to Greenfield Village in 1928. It is located next to the Clinton Inn, where it is now used to house horses and other Village livestock.

The *Ford Barn (below)* was built in 1863 by Henry Ford's father, William, at Springwells Township, Michigan, across the road from the family homestead. In 1933 it was moved to the Chicago World's Fair where it formed part of the Ford exhibit in the *Century of Progress Exposition.* It housed demonstrations for making plastics and other materials from the meal of Asian soybeans. When the exposition closed, the barn was brought to Greenfield Village and re-erected in 1935.

Visitors to Greenfield Village are not necessarily restricted to the two-legged human variety. Migratory birds and wild animals frequently drop in to hobnob with the Village livestock.

III. Around the Village Green

Throughout the seventeenth, eighteenth, and nineteenth centuries, and well into the twentieth, the village green was the hub from which a village radiated. Here, clustered around green lawn and shaded by maples, elms, and oaks, was the village center: the shops, the inn or tavern, the post office, the village hall. Here, in many eastern and midwestern communities, was located the bandstand where the local brass band assembled on summer evenings to serenade the population. Here stood the village flagpole. Here could be seen the spiked Civil War cannon. A village green was as essential to any self-respecting town as were its schools, its bank, its doctor, and its lawyer.

Greenfield Village is a real village in that its structures, of widely varying dates, were carefully moved here from many different locations for preservation. From its central green extend the streets which lead to the residential areas, the homes of famous Americans, the craft shops, and the industrial sites.

Around the Green itself are those buildings which speak of bygone America: the *Martha-Mary Chapel (left)*, the *Waterford General Store*, the *Clinton Inn*, the *Town Hall (above)*, the *Logan County "Abe Lincoln" Courthouse*, the *Scotch Settlement School*. Not on the green, but near at hand, are *Dr. Howard's Office*, the *Phoenixville Post Office*, and the *Deluge Firehouse*. These structures and their services, make up the essential components necessary to carry on normal village life.

The chapel represents three basic rites of man's progression: christening, marriage, and death.

The inn is the symbol of travel and hospitality. Here is the traveler's haven of rest as well as shelter for himself and his beasts; the site of restorative food,

drink, and warmth; friendly companionship, talk, and news of the world.

The general store was America's supply depot, housing everything needed in the surrounding community from dry goods and tools to special foods, patent medicines, household materials, and harness. A daily meeting place, it was a center of the village's informal social life.

It was at the town hall that the villagers met in formal session to debate their local problems, to vote budgets and laws, and to elect their local officials. Here could be housed the mayor, the constable, the village or town clerk. A jail was an awesome part of many such halls. And, when village business was not pressing, local and traveling performing groups used the stage to entertain with song, dance, and melodrama.

In the courthouse real-life dramas of the day were enacted in criminal and civil actions. Fledgling lawyers gained experience and reputation. Local citizens learned the responsibilities of jury duty and dispensed justice to their fellowmen.

The schoolhouse represented learning, however limited it might be. Without the ability to read, write, and figure sums, no village child could be expected to take his place in the adult community. He could not take full part in church services; he could not vote; he could not successfully engage in business. A free public school education was a privilege and a requirement for all.

Church, inn, store, town hall, courthouse, school: These Village Green structures represent those special values which every resident of an American village cherished and held dear.

Clinton Inn was built in 1831 to serve as the first overnight stagecoach stop between Detroit and Chicago. This landmark from southeast Michigan was an important crossroads for freight and mail and a "jump-off" point for travelers.

The Inn provided local residents with a convivial meeting place. Its strategic location on the Old Sauk Trail, a corduroy road, accounted for much of its popularity. Men often gathered in the taproom for drinking and colorful conversation. The Sunday parlor of the building, which is restored to look as it did during the stagecoach days, is furnished with Classical Revival pieces from the 1830s, 1840s, and 1850s. The everyday parlor, which once served as a lobby and sitting room, is decorated with painted country furniture of the mid-nineteenth century.

Today's visitors to Greenfield Village can still enjoy *Clinton Inn's* hospitality while dining amid antiques.

The Abraham Lincoln Courthouse, built at Postville, Logan County, in 1840, was used by "Honest Abe" while he traveled the Illinois "mud circuit" as a young attorney. When court was not in session, this black walnut clapboard structure served the tiny community, now known as Lincoln, as a church and assembly hall.

Many of the furnishings in this building are original Lincoln association pieces. The wall clock made by John Birge, the mahogany Empire chairs, and the folding, swivel-top card table with brass paw feet are from Lincoln's Springfield, Illinois, home. The walnut corner cupboard was made by Lincoln and his father.

Abraham Lincoln (1809-1865), sixteenth President of the United States, was assassinated while sitting in a Victorian rocking chair (right) during a performance of Our American Cousin at Ford's Theater in Washington, D.C. The chair, his playbill, and the shawl brought to him on that fateful evening are displayed here.

The Village post office *(left and top)* was constructed in Phoenixville, Connecticut, during the 1830s for use as an apothecary shop. With the advent of local postal service in 1850, it was adapted to serve also as the town post office. The hand-stamped postmark "Greenfield Village" appears on all mail posted by Village visitors today at the desk which is part of the building's original furnishings. Special two-cent postage stamps *(left, middle)* were issued in 1929 commemorating the golden jubilee of Edison's electric light.

Dr. Alonson Bingley Howard (1823-1883) acquired in 1855 the simple one-room, Greek Revival schoolhouse *(above)* built at Tekonsha, Michigan, in 1839. He remodeled it and created a reception room, a laboratory, and a personal office. Dr. Howard's original equipment and medicinal formula books are contained within the building. Wooden kegs, which he painted and labeled for his herbal remedies and root extracts, stock the homeopathic laboratory.

Dr. Howard, in 1852, was one of the first to attend the new medical school at the University of Michigan. As a practicing physician, he enjoyed the high respect of the patients he served. This building is a tribute not only to him but to all of America's country doctors.

The mid-nineteenth-century merchandise of Elias A. Brown's general store from Minaville, New York, is displayed in this two-story frame building which was erected in 1854 at Waterford, Michigan. Visiting the general store was usually a weekly event for people living in rural areas. The store served as a meeting place for friends and a clubhouse for the loungers who swapped stories and talked politics out front in the summer, and around the potbellied stove in the winter. The storekeeper, an important man in town, knew the latest news and often served as the Justice of the Peace, Town Clerk, and Village Postmaster. Candy, sundries, and items created by Greenfield Village craftsmen make the *General Store* a favorite browsing spot.

In early American towns the village smith crafted many different products at his forge. Prior to the automobile, one of his chief tasks was the fashioning of horse-shoes for use by the farrier who fitted and applied them to his customers' horses. This blacksmith shop *(above and left),* one of two at Greenfield Village, is used for miscellaneous ironwork and for the shoe-ing of horses. The hard surface of the Village roads makes it necessary for the horses to be reshod every four to six weeks.

The mid-nineteenth-century *Deluge Firehouse (right)* was originally built in Newton, New Hampshire. An oval fire mark above the door is similar to the in-signia given by American insurance com-panies to their customers during the eighteenth and nineteenth centuries to in-dicate that a building was covered by their insurance. An old triangular fire gong which now stands beside the firehouse once summoned volunteer firemen to local catastrophes. Today, modern well-equipped volunteer fire companies still serve thousands of small communities across America.

65

Henry Ford was given his first watch on his thirteenth birthday. Fascinated by anything mechanical, the youth soon "took it apart and put it together again." Almost immediately he was in the watch repair business. "Henry had wheels in his head . . . every clock in the Ford house shuddered when it saw Henry coming!" When he founded Greenfield Village, his lifetime interest in clocks and watches led to the inclusion of three clock shops and a Swiss watchmaker's chalet.

The famous *Sir John Bennett Jewelry Store (below)* with its effigies of Gog and Magog was moved from London, England, where it had been established at 66 Cheapside Street in 1846. Every fifteen minutes visitors are delighted by the movements of the polychrome and gold-leaf figures as they strike a series of Westminster chimes. Inside the store, collections of English and European clocks and watches, a display of Victorian jewelry, and exquisite English silver and Sheffield plate are vivid reminders of the elegant life-style of nineteenth-century England and the Continent.

The Magill Jewelry Store (below), where sixteen-year-old Henry Ford obtained a part-time job repairing watches, was moved from 444 Baker Street, Detroit. Today it houses a vast collection of American clocks and watches, illustrating the scope of nineteenth-century clockmaking and the development of the mass production of watches.

The Grimm Jewelry Store, not illustrated, originally located on Michigan Avenue in Detroit, was often frequented by Henry Ford. It contains his personal watch collection as well as the watchmaker's bench on which he often worked after the building was installed at Greenfield Village.

The bracket clock *(right)* is marked "Andrew Billings, Poughkeepsie, N.Y., 1795." The mahogany case, labeled by the firm of Slover and Kortright, New York City, is beautifully decorated with painting and satinwood inlays. The clock's eight-day, spring-driven, one-hour-strike movement not only records the time, the day, and the date, but also the time of high and low tides and the lunar date. This beautiful piece was made for Cadwallader D. Colden, who was Mayor of New York from 1818 to 1820 and later was also elected to the New York State Senate and the United States Congress.

In 1871 Henry Ford began school at the red brick *Scotch Settlement Schoolhouse (left and top, right)* which was about one-and-a-half miles from his Dearborn Township home. The second school he attended was the white. clapboard *Miller School (above).* Here his mechanical and inventive nature became apparent when he and his classmates constructed a steam turbine, a waterwheel, and a forge to make castings.

Henry Ford believed that "Education is the greatest force in civilization." He, his wife Clara, and their son Edsel, founders of The Edison Institute, are shown with a group of schoolchildren *(below).*

IV. Craft Shop to Factory

Self-sufficiency, for a long time, was a way of life in America. In the earliest communities about the Eastern seaboard and its interior rivers, in the frontier villages, and on the isolated farms as settlement moved westward, every man was responsible for his own well-being and that of his family. He felled trees, he planted crops, he erected houses and outbuildings. He butchered. He sold his cash crops. He lumbered. He hunted and fished for food and furs.

Life for himself and for his family was a never-ending round of toil and physical discomfort as they strove to produce the necessities for existence. What he or his neighbors could not raise or fashion with their own hands, they often did without. A pail of water became a mirror. A length of tree trunk became a chair.

Gradually, as settlements increased in size and in wealth, specialists took over certain communal duties. A blacksmith forged tools and metal parts. A potter made jugs, jars, essential tableware. A cooper produced tubs, firkins, pails. A weaver took the farm wife's yarn and wove it into cloth.

Until the nineteenth century, America was basically a craft-oriented nation, with craftsmen and artisans working at home or in relatively small shops where hand action and water were the main sources of power. Under the apprenticeship system, America's youths were bound to serve master craftsmen until they had learned their chosen crafts and became journeymen workers. Then, to prove their worth, certain journeymen might produce their masterpieces and achieve the elite classification of master.

In the nineteenth century the developing use of controlled power spelled the end of a craft-oriented society. Steam powered the factories; water drove the turbines that then turned power gears and belts. Cheap mass-produced goods competed with the handcrafts, driving them from the marketplace both by abundance and price.

Improved transportation—via steamboats and trains—gradually carried factory products to customers miles away from the places where they were made. In return, they brought necessary raw materials for workers to fashion into the needed finished goods. America became a nation of consumers.

A lad's apprenticeship now was to a machine. Few craftsmen remained to produce masterpieces.

Technologically, the nation prospered. Socially, it could be said that it retrogressed. Girls and boys left farms for stultifying work in towns. Children were exploited and abused. The mill-town family was little more than a work-unit.

The Industrial Revolution—that time of change from man's hands to machine power—wrought wrongs and evils beyond comprehension. Yet, from this time of radical change, a new national pattern emerged. Today, this pattern still develops.

In Greenfield Village, the operating craft shops and the early factory and mill structures well illustrate the industrial changes that have shaped the face of today's America.

The *Hanks Silk Mill (left),* built by Rodney Hanks at Mansfield, Connecticut, in 1810, was the first power mill to produce silk in the United States. In 1931, the mill was moved to Greenfield Village where silk thread is still produced directly from cocoons. A nearby grove of mulberry trees provides food for the young silkworms.

By the 1800s there were some two thousand small shoe factories in America similar to the *Currier Shoe Shop (above and right, top)* which was built and operated by William Currier in Newton, New Hampshire, during the 1880s. Because of their size, the shops were referred to as "ten-footers" and were often located beside the shoemaker's home.

The *Kingston Cooper Shop (right and far right),* the oldest American craft shop in Greenfield Village, was built in 1785 at Kingston, New Hampshire. Various hand axes and cooper's tools are displayed near the large fireplace in which barrels were charred.

The Tintype Studio *(left and below)* is separated into three sections—a "primping" room for customers, a camera room, and a darkroom for processing tintypes. The camera room is equipped with posing chairs and historic cameras including a four-lens tintype model from the 1880s. Ambrotypes and daguerreotypes, as well as tintypes of visiting celebrities to Greenfield Village over the years *(right),* are displayed.

Kit Carson

Abraham Lincoln

Edward Everett Horton

Joe Louis

Mrs. Henry Ford, Miss Mary Ellen Plantiff, Mrs. Gaston Plantiff

Walt Disney

Thomas Clarkson Gordon

Jane Withers

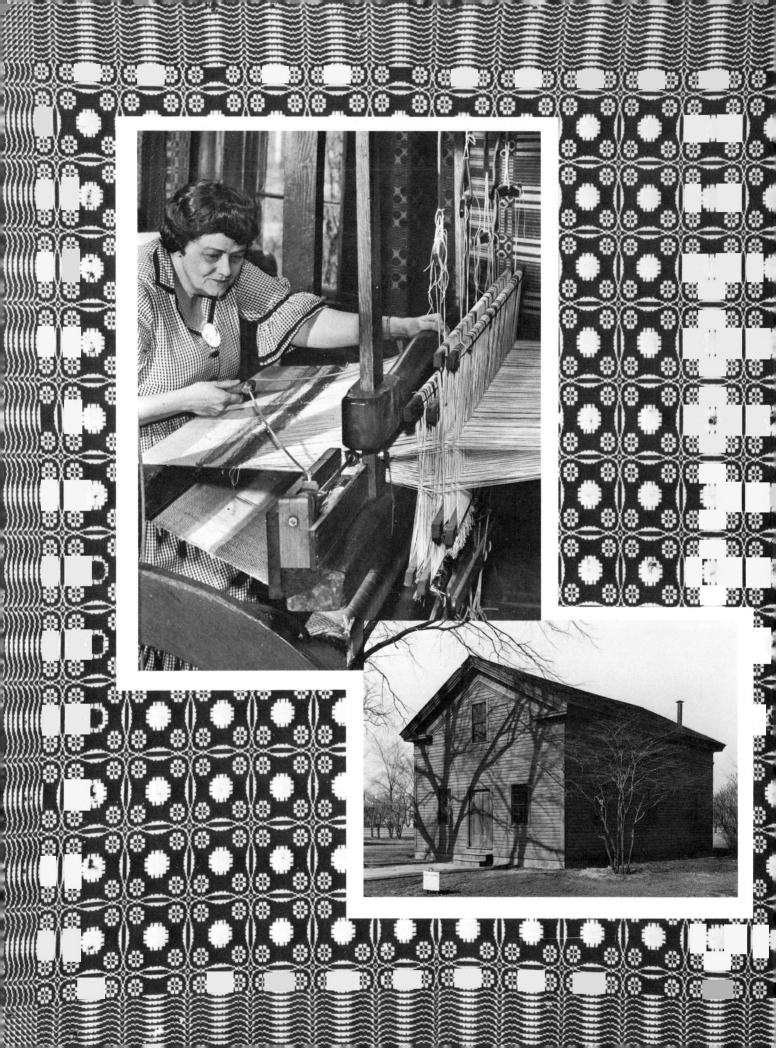

Demonstrations by the Greenfield Village craftsmen never cease to fascinate visitors for they recall a way of life long past. The costumed weaver *(left)* in a mid-nineteenth-century *Carding Mill* from Plymouth, Michigan, creates handsome scarves, bookmarks, and place mats. The *Cotton Gin Mill* (page 84) houses an unusual craft—the stenciling of hooked rug patterns *(below)*. These are created from a unique collection of original hooked rug stencils of zinc by an itinerant Biddeford, Maine, peddler, Edward Sands Frost (active 1870–1880).

The name of the Boston and Sandwich Glass Company is perpetuated by the *Sandwich Glass Plant* rebuilt in Greenfield Village with surviving bricks and wooden framework taken from the original 1825 factory at Sandwich, Massachusetts. In this building skilled craftsmen blow glass using the techniques of nineteenth-century gaffers. The cut glass lamp and lacy pressed glass covered dish are part of a comprehensive collection of Sandwich products displayed in the Museum.

Above: The original corporate and work records for the Boston and Sandwich Glass Company are preserved in the Henry Ford Museum Research Library.

The Martinsville Cider Mill (above), with its late nine-teenth-century machinery, is used by Village craftsmen to demonstrate the production of apple cider.

In his Sharpsburg, Pennsylvania, brick house *(lower left)* built in 1854, H. J. Heinz produced the first of his more than "57 Varieties." During the 1860s, this pioneer food preservationist manufactured horseradish and distributed it to nearby Pittsburgh grocers. This building, used as the Heinz factory from 1869 to 1875, was opened in 1904 as a company museum. The desk, chairs, and advertising materials on display in this home belonged to the Heinz family.

Edward Loranger constructed his *Gristmill (below)* on Stony Creek near Monroe, Michigan, in 1832. In the eighteenth and nineteenth centuries every village of any size supported a mill, and local farmers came by ox cart, pack horse or on foot, from miles around, carrying grain to be ground into flour. The original land grant for this water-powered mill, signed by John Quincy Adams in 1825, is displayed in the building.

The Tripp Sawmill (above), built in 1855 at Tipton, Michigan, is an unusual nineteenth-century type, in that it uses a vertical saw *(right).* It is powered by a steam engine on the first floor.

The gate of the "up-and-down" sawmill *(left, top)* is from John Spofford's early mill built at Georgetown, Massachusetts, in 1682. During the nineteenth century, mills of this early type were generally superseded by those using circular saws.

After 1850, circular sawmills were common in Michigan and other lumbering areas across America. The circular saw *(right)* which was once used at Stony Creek in Monroe, Michigan, easily proved its superiority over the earlier up-and-down type. The sprawling, weathered *Stony Creek Sawmill (below)* is a picturesque addition to Greenfield Village's portrayal of nineteenth-century industrial America.

Rice was usually threshed in mills similar to the *Fairfield Rice Mill (left)* rather than by portable threshing machines used on most other grains. Such structures were found in South Carolina and other rice-growing sections of the old South.

The early nineteenth-century *Cotton Gin Mill (center)* from "Richmond Hill," Henry Ford's plantation in Georgia, once housed cotton gins used for separating the seeds from cotton.

The heavy machinery preserved in the *Harahan Sugar Mill (right)* from the "Bourbon Plantation" near Harahan, Louisiana, was used for crushing cane in the manufacture of sugar and molasses. Sugar production was a major industry and basic factor in the southern economy during the mid-1800s.

Armington & Sims Machine Shop (above) contains the records, patterns, and machines of that Rhode Island firm which manufactured high-speed steam engines *(near right, top)* for the Edison Illuminating Companies during the 1880s. Greenfield Village craftsmen now use this building for the restoration of antique machinery.

A 120-horsepower *Walking Beam Engine (left, middle)*, built about 1845, and its boiler, were used at the Vaucluse Gold Mine in Orange County, Virginia, until the Civil War. They were originally imported from Cornwall, England.

The eighteenth-century *Haycock Boiler (left, bottom)* was used at the J. Charlesworth Colliery at Wakefield, Yorkshire, England.

A steam engine built by the Stillman-Allen Novelty Works of Buffalo, New York, in 1840, is the power plant for Greenfield Village's *Print Shop (far right, top)*. Steam from a nearby upright boiler powers this horizontal engine, one of the first in America.

Built in 1836, the Gothic design *Walking Beam Engine (right, bottom)* was used until 1929 in the shop of John S. Lewis and Brothers, Philadelphia, Pennsylvania.

A brick machine shop was erected in 1878 to enlarge and replace the small shop contained in the Edison laboratory. In the interior *(left, bottom)* the world's first experimental electric power generating station began operating on December 31, 1879, when Edison demonstrated his incandescent lamp and electrical engineering system for the first time. Witnessing this spectacle were over three thousand people who had come to Menlo Park, New Jersey, for the occasion. After this practical application of electricity for the production of heat, light, power, and communication, commercial electrical generating stations were built in major cities across the United States.

The Edison Illuminating Company, Station "A" (left), was the first establishment to provide electricity for the City of Detroit. In this power plant, which opened in 1886, Henry Ford eventually achieved the status of Chief Engineer. While acting in that capacity, he was chosen to attend the Company's annual convention in 1896 at New York, where he first met Thomas Alva Edison. Years later Ford established Greenfield Village and the Henry Ford Museum, naming them *The Edison Institute* in honor of his friend and mentor, the man he felt assured was one of the most creative geniuses the world had ever seen.

The Edison Laboratory from Fort Myers, Florida *(below),* was used by the inventor as a winter workshop beginning in 1884. Here Edison undertook numerous experiments in botanical science and during World War I developed a formula for producing synthetic rubber from the goldenrod plant. The building is preserved with its original equipment and furnishings, including Mr. Edison's mahogany desk, pine chair, drafting table mounted on wooden horses, and stool.

Although handcrafted wagons were the chief product of his *Carriage Shop (below)*, Israel Biddle Richart also produced farm implements and furniture. A wheelwright from McEvansville, Pennsylvania, Richart established his business at Macon, Michigan, in 1851.

An angry conductor on the Grand Trunk Railroad running between Detroit and Port Huron in 1863 threw young Tom Edison off the train at the Smiths Creek, Michigan, depot *(above, left)*. Tom, a newsboy and "candy butcher," had accidentally set the baggage car afire while conducting a chemical experiment. The building, a combination stationmaster's home and depot, is typical of country railroad stations of the second half of the nineteenth century.

The 1873 Mason-Fairlie funnel-stack steam locomotive *Torch Lake (left and below)* was used in the ore mines of Michigan's Keeweenaw Peninsula. It now provides a nostalgic ride for early railroad buffs.

At the age of thirty-three, Henry Ford built his first automobile which he called the "Quadricycle." It is shown (right) outside of his backyard shop originally located at 58 Bagley Avenue, Detroit. Mr. Ford test-drove the car, which was belt-driven by a two-cylinder, three-horsepower rear engine, very early on the morning of June 4, 1896. The success of his first gasoline automobile gave him the confidence necessary to continue his automotive experiments which ultimately led to the founding of the Ford Motor Company.

The first Ford Motor Company factory, originally located on Mack Avenue in Detroit, was used for assembly purposes only. All component parts were manufactured elsewhere and brought to the plant on horse-drawn hayracks. Men worked on four cars at a time and hoped to assemble fifteen cars a day. Early automobiles in front of the reconstructed building (below) are the 1902 prototype Ford Runabout (right), the 1903 Model A Runabout (center), and the 1905 Model F Runabout (left). From such modest beginnings, the Ford Motor Company grew rapidly. The Highland Park plant (right) was built in 1910 for the construction of the famous Model T. The moving assembly line was first introduced here, and by 1913 one thousand cars a day were being produced. At this plant, on January 12, 1914, Henry Ford made his historic announcement of the introduction of the revolutionary five-dollar-a-day wage.

V. Special Events

American history comes to life at Greenfield Village in numerous ways throughout the year. Special events at the annual *Country Fair* include an exhibition presented by members of the Early American Steam Engine Club *(far left, top)* and the 4-H horse show *(near left)*. The annual *Rug Hooking Bee and Exhibition (lower left)* attracts colorful entries from across the entire United States. Gatherings of this type were a common occurrence in the rural United States during the nineteenth century.

Sound, smoke, and the acrid odor of gunpowder punctuate the activities at the annual *Muzzle Loaders' Festival (right)* where costumed frontiersmen, Indians, British Redcoats, and Civil War volunteers test their skill under rules established by the National Muzzle Loading Rifle Association. The staccato blasts of antique rifles, a Gatling gun, and authentic Civil War cannon re-create America's earlier days. The *Let Freedom Ring* ceremony *(below)* every Fourth of July observes with dignity, simple pageantry, and commemorative remarks, the birth of America. Young people in Colonial garb re-enact the signing of the Declaration of Independence.

The Old Car Festival, a panorama of the history of America's early motoring days, unfolds as hundreds of pre-1925 cars test the mettle of both drivers and machines in a series of races and contests. The vintage vehicles are also judged on the authenticity of their restoration. Since the annual *Old Car Festival* is recognized as one of the largest and finest events of its kind in the country, the awards are highly prized by automotive buffs. The festive activities begin with a parade through the streets of Greenfield Village. A special exhibition of historic cars from the Henry Ford Museum's permanent collection tells the story of the development of the American automobile.

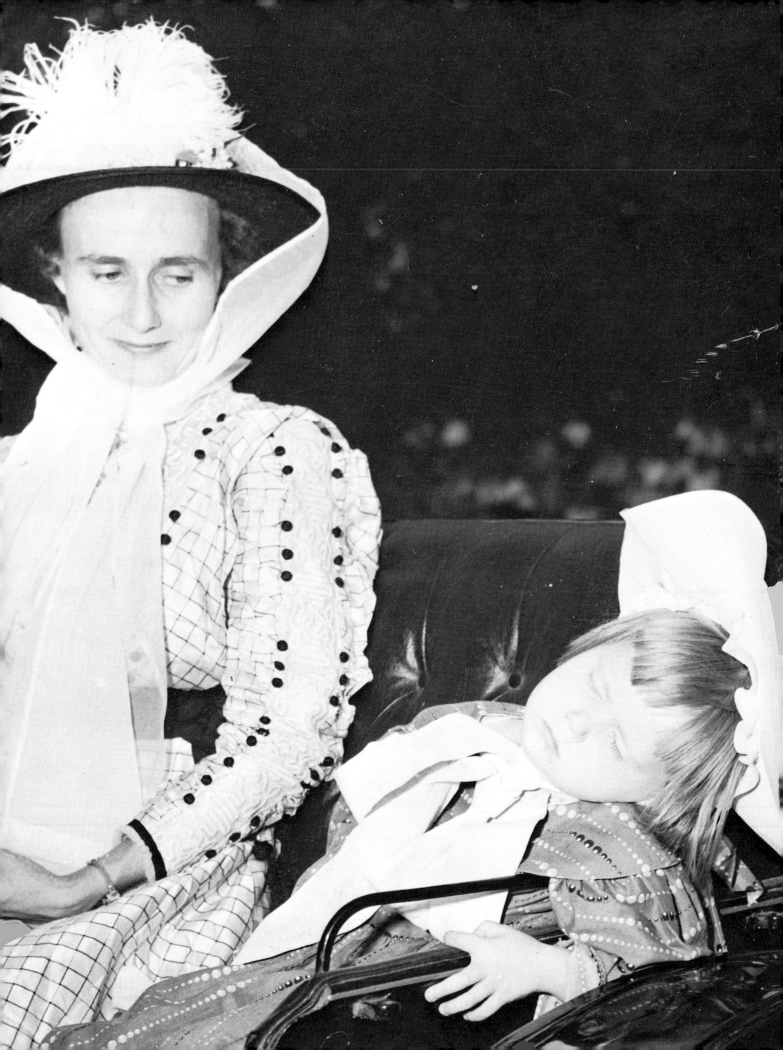

Henry Ford Museum

Preserving America's Heritage

The Henry Ford Museum

Crown Publishers, Inc.   New York

Entrance hall of the Henry Ford Museum.

Henry Ford Museum

Introduction by
Robert G. Wheeler,
Vice-President,
Research and Interpretation

World-famous guests at the dedication of Greenfield Village and the Henry Ford Museum on October 21, 1929, gathered in the entrance galleries of the Museum building at 6:15 P.M. for a formal banquet, with Owen D. Young as Toastmaster. The chambers in which they were seated were lighted by candles. Buildings in the nearby Village were illuminated by gas. Graham Mc-Namee broadcast the proceedings.

Thomas Alva Edison, guest of honor on this momentous occasion, left the dinner and was driven in a horse-drawn carriage to his Menlo Park Laboratory, painstakingly removed from its original site in New Jersey for preservation at Greenfield Village. Here, in the presence of President Herbert Hoover and Henry Ford, he re-enacted that great moment when he, fifty years earlier, had lighted his first electric lamp. Immediately, the Museum's crystal chandeliers blazed with electric light, as did the Village houses. All across the nation and indeed, throughout the world, darkened houses were lighted. This was the moment of Light's Golden Jubilee!

At the entrance to the Museum, enclosed in glass, is a cornerstone, dedicated one year earlier, on September 27, 1928. To symbolize the union of agriculture and industry, Mr. Edison had thrust Luther Burbank's spade into the wet cement, imprinted his own footsteps, and inscribed his name and the date.

The Henry Ford Museum is composed of three distinct areas under one roof. At the front, housed in exact reproductions of Philadelphia's Independence Hall, Carpenter's Hall, and the Old City Hall, are the American Decorative Arts Galleries. Here, superb collections of furniture, ceramics, glass, pewter, silver, and textiles illustrate the development and use of the decorative arts in America from the Pilgrim period to the late nineteenth century.

Thomas Alva Edison and Henry Ford at the laying of the cornerstone for the Henry Ford Museum, September 27, 1928.

Entrance to the Museum is through an exact replica of Independence Hall. One of the most treasured pieces in the Decorative Arts Galleries is the original Speaker's chair carved by Thomas Affleck (1740-1795) and used in that historic structure.

Painting by Irving Bacon of the banquet held on October 21, 1929, celebrating the fiftieth anniversary of Edison's creation of the incandescent lamp.

Behind is the great Mechanical Arts Hall with its collections—agriculture, home arts and crafts, industrial machinery, steam and electric power, lighting, communication, and transportation.

Uniting these two units is the Street of Early American Shops, where twenty-two buildings stocked with appropriate period collections represent America's eighteenth- and nineteenth-century craft shops and stores.

It could well be said that the Mechanical Arts Hall contains the tools with which America's artisans and farmers worked. The Street of Shops illustrates the surroundings in which so many of them worked with these tools, or sold the products of their hands. In the Decorative Arts Galleries are the products of their labor and the evidences of their daily lives.

Truly, the Henry Ford Museum is a general museum of American history housed in the most American of buildings. Here, with collections matchless in both depth and scope, is the story of America's growth, its inventive genius, the development of its tastes and modes. Any one section of this Museum, be it agriculture, power, transportation, communication, or furniture, is a fascinating history of the American people—their yearnings, their explorations, their accomplishments.

Complementing the collections of the Museum are: a specialized Research Library concentrating upon technical works relating to all the collections, the Ford Archives, a full theater program of America's nineteenth-century drama and of early twentieth-century films, a special exhibitions program, and an Adult Education Program.

Both the Henry Ford Museum and Greenfield Village have individual purposes for being. In the Museum, in unique installations, are the artifacts demonstrating America's movement over a span of three centuries. Little or nothing is missing. The story lines are so complete that they include such diverse elements as telephones, cameras, clocks and watches, refrigerators, stoves, guns, and musical instruments. The in-depth exhibits must be seen to be comprehended.

Greenfield Village with its one hundred structures brought together from many areas of our nation, on the other hand, illustrates in period settings how Americans lived and worked over this period. Nowhere else in the world does such a combination of indoor-outdoor museum complex exist.

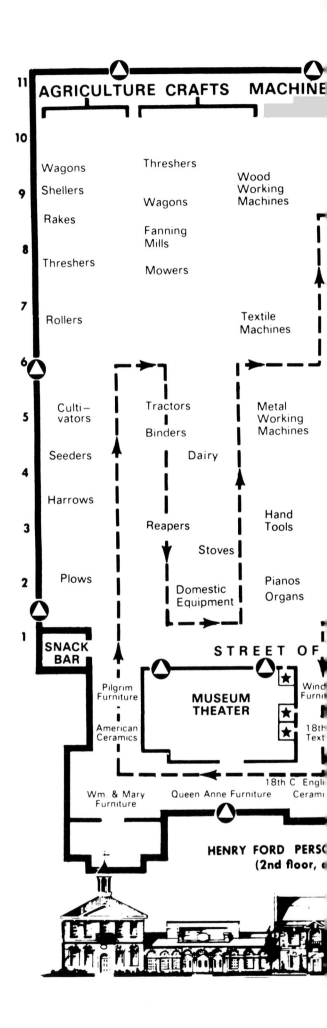

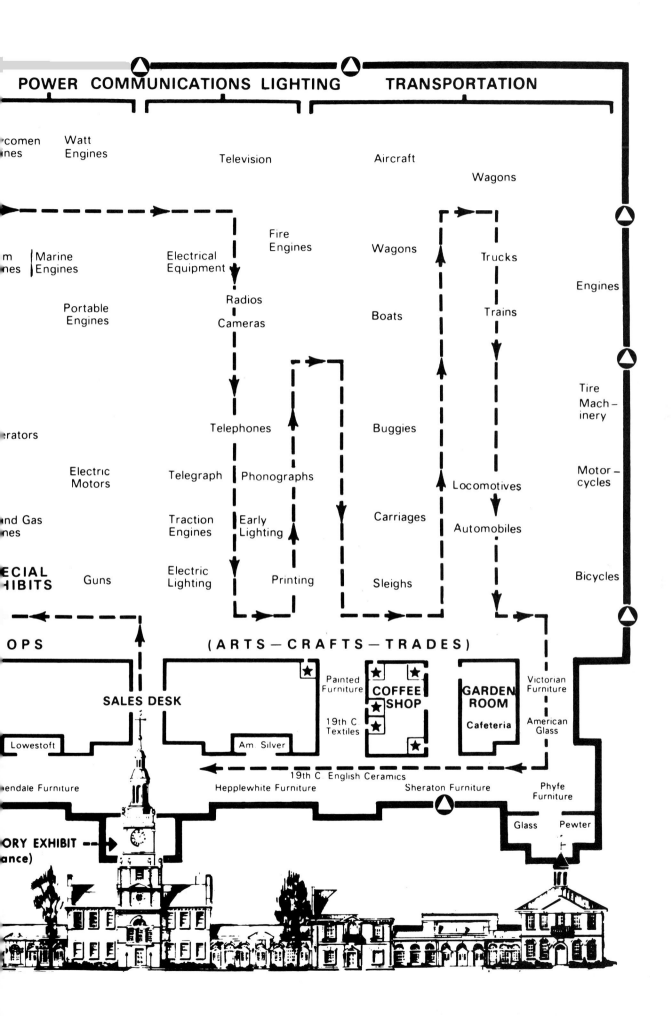

POWER COMMUNICATIONS LIGHTING   TRANSPORTATION

comen
nes   Watt
                   Engines
                                      Television   Aircraft
                                                                        Wagons

m   Marine   Electrical   Fire
nes   Engines   Equipment   Engines   Wagons   Trucks
                                                                                              Engines
                                      Radios
               Portable   Boats   Trains
               Engines   Cameras

                                                                                              Tire
                                                                                              Mach-
                                                                                              inery

rators   Telephones   Buggies

                                                                                              Motor-
               Electric   Telegraph   Phonographs   cycles
               Motors   Locomotives

nd Gas   Traction   Early   Carriages   Automobiles
nes   Engines   Lighting

ECIAL   Bicycles
IBITS   Guns   Electric   Printing   Sleighs
                              Lighting

OPS

(ARTS — CRAFTS — TRADES)

                                              ★
                                    Painted   ★   ★
                      SALES DESK   Furniture COFFEE   GARDEN   Victorian
                                              ★SHOP   ROOM   Furniture

                                                                            American
Lowestoft   Am. Silver 19th C.   Cafeteria   Glass
                                              ★Textiles
                                              ★

endale Furniture   ★
                      19th C. English Ceramics   Phyfe
               Hepplewhite Furniture   Sheraton Furniture   Furniture

ORY EXHIBIT   Glass   Pewter
ance)

I. Decorative Arts Galleries
1. Furniture

The furniture collections, which include virtually all the existing forms and styles made in America from the seventeenth through the nineteenth centuries, are arranged in the Decorative Arts Galleries as a chronological study collection, interspersed with numerous period

room settings. Henry Ford's interest in obtaining objects originally owned by the people who were instrumental in the founding and development of America is demonstrated by the inclusion of many pieces of furniture which personally belonged to George Washington, John Hancock, Benjamin Franklin, Abraham Lincoln, Ulysses S. Grant, and countless others. The products of noted cabinetmakers and of various cabinetmaking centers are also represented.

Left: The massive, oak, New England armchair, 1640–1650, is called a Brewster chair because William Brewster, the Pilgrim leader, owned a similar turned piece with spindles under both the seat and arms.

Above: The Massachusetts oak, pine, and maple table, with ebonized bobbin-turned stretchers, is typical of the American phase of the Cromwellian style (1680–1700). The half-octagon-shaped Massachusetts Bible box of oak and pine is decorated with carving and dated 1670.

Right: Mary Ball Washington, mother of George Washington, once owned this burl walnut-veneered William and Mary high chest of drawers (1700–1720). It was exhibited at the Chicago World's Fair in 1893, where it sparked a renewal of interest in objects associated with America's past.

Numerous new design elements were introduced during the American Queen Anne period, 1720–1755. Outstanding characteristics of the Queen Anne style were solid vase-shaped splats in the backs of chairs and cabriole legs usually terminating in pad feet. Although carved shells and arched panels were much used as embellishments, the overall effect was one of simplicity when compared to the more massively proportioned Pilgrim or William and Mary furniture.

Left and Center: The tile-top Queen Anne mixing table with cabriole legs and pad feet, 1720–1740, is the larger of two known. Biblical scenes are depicted on the twenty blue and white Delft tiles set into the top of this unusual piece.

Right: The japanned, scrolled looking glass, 1735–1745, was originally owned by Isaac Van Keuren in New York and probably was decorated by Gerardus Duyckinck, Sr., a well-known artisan of the day.

Below: Solomon Fussell (1700–1762), a cabinetmaker of Philadelphia, Pennsylvania, made this walnut side chair around 1750, one of a pair, for Benjamin Franklin (1706–1790).

The designs of Thomas Chippendale, a London cabinetmaker, were widely adapted and interpreted by American craftsmen during the last half of the eighteenth century. Characteristic features of the style are cabriole legs with claw and ball feet, carved shells, tendrils and leafage, fluted quarter columns, gadrooning, and the predominant use of richly figured, imported mahogany.

Far left: The elaborately carved mahogany Philadelphia-style high chest of drawers was made in Maryland about 1760.

Center, top: Hosea Dugliss of New York City labeled the walnut, parcel gilded and gesso looking glass, 1798–1820.

Left, below: Of Pennsylvania origin, the mahogany tilt-top table with piecrust edge dates between 1760 and 1780.

Below: The mahogany Chippendale open armchair, with carved eagles at the arms, was made in Massachusetts about 1750.

Federal style furniture, created between 1785 and 1820, expressed the American interpretation of the classical English designs of Robert Adam, George Hepplewhite, Thomas Sheraton, and numerous others. The characteristics of this style are straight lines, the use of inlay and bandings for decorative motifs, and the introduction of a tapered leg and foot.

Below: This leather-upholstered Sheraton armchair is one of a large set made in 1797 by George Bright (1726–1805) for use in the Old State House, Boston, Massachusetts.

Right, bottom: The Hepplewhite mahogany desk with open shelves, circa 1790, is similar to an example used by George Washington in the Federal Hall at New York.

Right, top: The early nineteenth-century bronze, marble, and Wedgwood mantel ornament is topped by figures of George Washington, "Father of His Country," and an eagle, symbolic of infant America.

Painting, gilding, and stenciling were popular decorative techniques employed by late eighteenth- and early nineteenth-century craftsmen to enrich their furniture.

Above: The mahogany piano, inlaid with satinwood and brass, is further enhanced with green and gilt stenciling. The case is by Duncan Phyfe (1768–1854) and the works are by Gibson & Davis (working 1801-1820 at New York City).

Below: Made in Baltimore, Maryland, by Thomas Renshaw, the settee and two matching side chairs were decorated by John Barnhart, circa 1815.

Right: Gilded pine girandole mirrors with either concave or convex glasses were popular embellishments of early nineteenth-century homes.

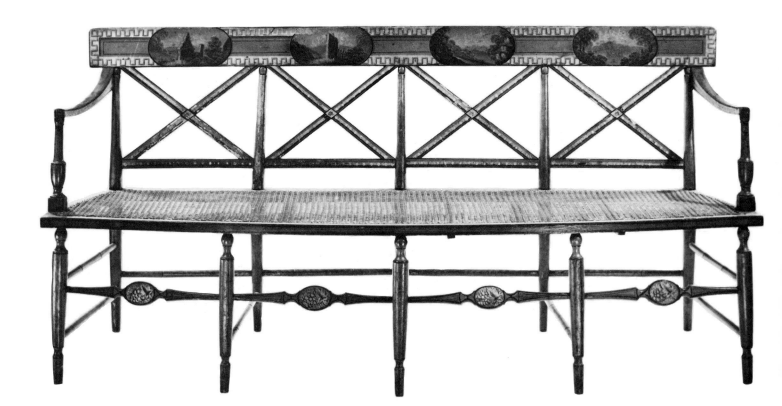

Early in the nineteenth century, the Hepplewhite and Sheraton styles evolved into the Empire style.

Below: The couch, carved, circa 1810, in Salem, Massachusetts, by Samuel McIntire (1757–1811), illustrates Grecian influence in the scrolled ends and Roman influence in the flared or saber legs.

Bottom: This Empire room setting exhibits classical furniture forms, several of which were made by the renowned New York cabinetmaker Duncan Phyfe.

Right: Made in Philadelphia by Joseph B. Barry and Sons, circa 1820, the large mahogany veneered breakfront-desk was used by Andrew Jackson at The Hermitage. Classical devices on this piece are the gargoyle figures on the corner columns and the brass animal-paw feet.

115

Because the American Victorian period lasted almost sixty years—from 1840 through 1900—there are many substyles which are considered by scholars as movements within themselves. The last phase of the Late Classical Movement during the 1840s was based upon large, simple, scrolled furniture with elegantly veneered or walnut surfaces. The ornate exuberance of the Rococo Revival, popular during the 1850s and early 1860s, contrasts with the quiet restraint of the flat incised carving and inlays of the Renaissance Revival of the 1860s and 1870s.

Left: The New York furniture firm of John Henry Belter (1804–1863) supplied Abraham Lincoln with this elaborate laminated "turtle top" table. It is part of a large suite of parlor furniture used in Lincoln's Springfield, Illinois, home.

Right: Though many critics decried chairs constructed in the Renaissance Revival style as "instruments of torture," they were immensely popular and provided nouveau riche American families with a visual means of displaying their wealth.

Many Germans emigrated from the Old World to America during the eighteenth and early nineteenth centuries in an attempt to secure for themselves the political and religious freedoms permitted in the New World. Settling primarily in southeastern Pennsylvania, they clung tenaciously to the middle-European traditions of their homeland. Whether applied to furniture or pottery, Pennsylvania-German designs are strong and robust. Favorite motifs include the tulip, heart, birds, stars, and other floral and animal forms. The *schrank* or wardrobe *(below)* with its painted and marbelized decoration was made in Lancaster County about 1790. During the nineteenth century, many other European groups seeking religious freedom settled in numerous areas along the frontier. Furniture makers in these settlements produced distinctive styles of their own. A member of the Ohio communal group of Zoarites made, circa 1825, the three-legged walnut table *(center)*. Nineteenth-century Shaker boxes are stacked on it. Furnishings crafted by members of the Shaker sect *(far right, top)* in New Hampshire and New York, as well as in other states, are shown both in the Decorative Arts Galleries and in the Street of Shops.

The most popular chair in America—the Windsor—was used in the humble as well as the more elegant homes of the eighteenth century. Benjamin Franklin signed the Declaration of Independence while sitting in a bow-back Windsor armchair. Thomas Jefferson wrote the historic document on a swivel-based writing-arm Windsor of his own design. During the mid-nineteenth century, simple, inexpensive, painted chairs were confined to rural homes. At first, they were handcrafted; later, they were mass-produced in vast quantities by chairmaking firms who sold and shipped them in wholesale, ready-to-assemble lots. The late eighteenth-century Rhode Island bow-back settee *(lower right)* is a rare Windsor form.

120

The horological collection consists of over three thousand individual clocks and watches. Elaborate timekeeping devices which also indicate the sign of the zodiac, the solar cycle, and the epact or phases of the moon, dramatically contrast with the ordinary late nineteenth-century kitchen clocks. Most of the outstanding American clockmakers from the eighteenth through the twentieth centuries are represented in this comprehensive collection.

Far left: Japanned tall-case clock. Made by Gawen Brown, Boston, Massachusetts, dated 1766. Eight-day brass movement with hour strike.

Middle left: Tall-case clock in Queen Anne style. Made by Thomas Norton, Rising Sun, Maryland, circa 1790. Steel and brass eight-day movement with brass and pewter dial.

Left, top: Banjo timepiece. Made by Aaron Willard, Boston, Massachusetts, circa 1820. The banjo-style timepiece was invented in 1802 by Aaron's brother, Simon Willard.

Left, bottom: Shelf or dwarf tall-case clock made in 1806 by B. S. Young, while he was a member of the Shaker community at Watervliet, New York. Eight-day brass movement with alarm.

Right, top: Shelf clock. Made by David Wood, Newburyport, Massachusetts, circa 1810. Eight-day brass movement.

Right, center: Pillar and Scroll shelf clock with outside escapement. Made by Eli Terry, Plymouth, Connecticut, circa 1820. Thirty-hour wood movement with hour strike.

Right, bottom: Acorn mantel clock. Made by Forestville Manufacturing Company, Bristol, Connecticut, circa 1848. The picture on the painted tablet is the home of J. C. Brown, president of the company.

Far right: Tall-case clock in Chippendale style. The case was made by Thomas Affleck (died 1795), Philadelphia, Pennsylvania. Robert Shearman made the eight-day brass movement with hour strike. Painted dial.

2. Clocks

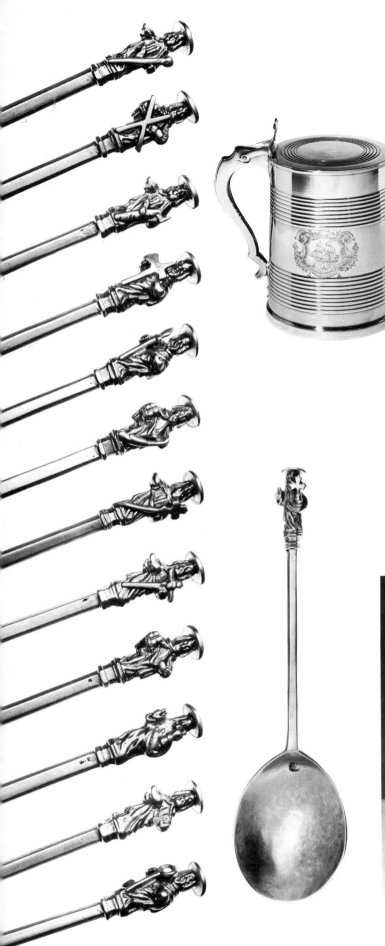

The silver collection illustrates the changing styles of American craftsmanship from the seventeenth through the revivalistic nineteenth century. Many historic names and events are recorded by pieces in the collection.

Far and lower left: The complete set of James I Apostle spoons, by the unknown maker I. S., London (1617–1618), is known as the Sulhamstead set. The gilded figures that top the spoon handles show the apostolic emblems according to the Germanic system.

Left: The flat-top banded tankard was created by Joseph Lownes, circa 1790, a Philadelphia craftsman.

Below: The custom of drinking tea and coffee provided Colonials with an opportunity for displaying their wealth. Elaborate coffeepots like the example by Joseph Anthony, Jr., circa 1785, the waste bowl by Joseph Richardson, circa 1775, and the covered sugar bowl by William Hollingshead, circa 1780, all Philadelphia craftsmen, were certain to impress neighbors.

Right: The rococo silver coffeepot was made circa 1760 at Boston, Massachusetts, by Paul Revere (1735–1818), the man immortalized in Henry Wadsworth Longfellow's "Paul Revere's Ride."

Because gold is one of the most precious of metals, in America it was usually fashioned into objects of personal decoration rather than into utilitarian pieces. The gold collection is comprised of three major groups—Masonic jewels, mourning jewelry, and decorative adornments. The Museum collection of mourning jewelry, tokens of remembrance given at funerals, is the word's largest and includes several marked rings. Coral and bells (an infant's rattle); a plain gold wedding band given by "Baron" Henry William Stiegel to Elizabeth Holtz during their marriage ceremony in Roxborough, Pennsylvania, on October 24, 1758; and spectacles are some of the more unusual items in the gold collection.

Above: Masonic jewel given in 1855 to Master Samuel L. Fowle of East Boston, Massachusetts.

Near right, top: Masonic jewel marked "T. H.," United States, early nineteenth century.

Near right, center: Masonic jewel elaborately engraved by Francis Shallus, Philadelphia, Pennsylvania, 1812.

Near right, bottom: Group of mourning jewelry from the funeral of Stephen van Rensselaer who died at New York in 1786. The rings are marked by Jacob Boelen II (1733–1786) of New York.

Far right, top: Pair of spectacles by James McAllister, Philadelphia, circa 1840, in their original red leather case.

Far right, bottom: Gold-washed, silver coffee service by Edwin Stebbins & Company, New York, circa 1850.

124

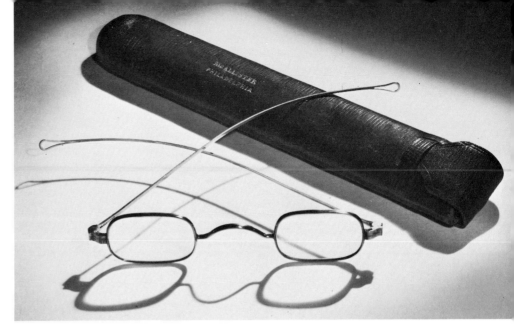

Left: Jewelry originally made for Abigail Matson Coults of Old Lyme, Connecticut, circa 1770. Brooch marked by Ambrose Ward (1735–1809), New Haven, Connecticut.

Objects made from the minor metals, while generally not as sophisticated as those crafted from gold or silver, are equally important in illustrating American history. Unusual examples are the pair of brass andirons and the pewter communion service.

Above: Pewter communion service by Johann Christoph Heyne, Lancaster, Pennsylvania, made for the Canadochly Lutheran Church, York County, Pennsylvania, 1765.

Left, top: Cast iron teakettle, United States, circa 1825.

Left, center: Bell metal skimmer marked by William Barton, New York State, circa 1825.

Bottom: Connecticut River Valley pewter including such makers as the Danforth family *(left case);* Thomas Danforth Boardman and Company *(center case);* Jacob Whitmore, Amos Treadway, Samuel Pierce, Richard Lee, Sr. and Jr., and Ebenezer Southmayd *(right case).*

Below: Brass andirons, Revere-type, Boston, Massachusetts, circa 1780.

Near right: Copper teakettle marked by Best and Russell, Canton, Ohio, circa 1820.

Far right: Decorative wrought iron candle trammel, Pennsylvania-German, circa 1750.

Above: Miniature of James Earle by Robert Field, dated 1802, Annapolis, Maryland. Watercolor on ivory.

Above: Unknown man painted by Joseph Badger, circa 1755, Boston, Massachusetts. Oil on canvas.

4. Painting and Sculpture

Portrait painting—the art of taking a likeness—has been practiced in America since Pilgrim times. Portraits in the collection date from 1700 through the nineteenth century, and were painted by such artists as Gerret Duyckinck, John Watson, John Wollaston, Ralph Earl, Jeremiah Theus, Chester Harding, and many others. The artists represented in a large group of miniature portraits include Edward Greene Malbone, Benjamin Trott, Nathaniel Rogers, Anna Claypoole Peale, Charles Fraser, Thomas Seir Cummings, John Wesley Jarvis, Henry Benbridge, and Thomas Sully.

Center left, top: Miniature of Thomas Ladson Ferguson by Charles Willson Peale, circa 1790, Philadelphia, Pennsylvania. Watercolor on ivory.

Near left, top: Miniature of an unknown man by John Ramage, circa 1780, New York City. Watercolor on ivory.

Far left, bottom: Miss Huysche by Charles Bridges, circa 1735, South Carolina. Oil on canvas.

Above: John Duncan by Thomas McIlworth, circa 1757, New York City. Oil on canvas. Of special interest is the original intricately carved gilt gesso frame on this painting.

Right, bottom: Maria Franklin, first wife of DeWitt Clinton, Governor of New York, by Ezra Ames, circa 1810, Albany, New York. Oil on canavs.

Above: General Henry Dearborn, painted by Gilbert Stuart, circa 1810, New York City. Oil on canvas.

Above: Oil portrait of William Moore signed and dated by Charles Peale Polk, 1797, Baltimore, Maryland.

Near right, top and bottom: Plaster busts of George Washington and Benjamin Franklin by Jean Antoine Houdon, circa 1775, France.

Far right, top: Bronze sculpture, *The Rattlesnake,* by Frederic Remington (1861–1909), cast by the Roman Bronze Works, New York City.

Far right, bottom: Plaster sculpture, *The Council of War* among Grant, Lincoln, and Stanton, by John Rogers, circa 1875, New York City. John Rogers was one of the very first sculptors to sell to the public multiple plaster copies of his original bronzes. Most "Rogers Groups" are three-dimensional depictions similar in effect to the mid-Victorian people and the mid-Victorian scenes that are so frequently the subjects of Currier and Ives prints.

130

5. Ceramics

The wives of prosperous colonists who wished to prove their superior position in the community imported their pottery and porcelain from England, the Continent, and the Orient. Makers of American tableware concentrated on functionalism, and their products contrasted sharply with European-made pieces where style and quality were the prime considerations.

Far left: The painted New England Queen Anne corner cupboard, circa 1765, displays examples of English eighteenth-century redware, creamware, Delft, and glass. The types of pottery shown here were listed in an advertisement in the New York *Gazette,* 1771.

Near left, top: The early eighteenth-century salt glaze covered honey jar in the form of a bear is English, and probably was brought to America by an immigrant family or purchased from an Atlantic seaboard merchant.

Near left, bottom: The monumental pistol-handled Chinese export porcelain urn, circa 1785, one of a pair, belonged to the famed Winthrop family of Boston, Massachusetts.

Below: The blue and white soft-paste porcelain pitcher was made at Caughley, Shropshire, England, circa 1775.

Right and below: The shell-shaped teapot with straw-berry decoration and the large platter with blue trans-fer-printed Arms of Pennsylvania were made at Staffordshire, England, about 1825.

Above: The Parian eagle vase was manufactured by the U.S. Pottery Company at Bennington, Vermont, circa 1850.

Right, top: The William Ellis Tucker Factory at Philadelphia produced, circa 1830, the French-style pitcher with landscape scene.

Right: Made by Knowles, Taylor, and Knowles at East Liverpool, Ohio, circa 1890, the "Lotus Ware" Belleek porcelain vase is ornately painted and gilded.

Abigail Adams, wife of the first President to live in the White House, established a tradition when she ordered china for the new Executive Mansion from the French firm of Sèvres. An 1826 Act of Congress decreed that all equipment for the President's House must be native to America when feasible, but it was not until 1917 that Mrs. Woodrow Wilson selected an American firm, Lenox of Trenton, New Jersey, to supply the White House tableware.

Right: An order placed in China by the Society of the Cincinnati for a dinner service as a gift for George Washington was received in 1786. The plate, one of three hundred pieces in the set of porcelain, is centered with the emblem of the Society held by the Angel of Fame and framed with a blue Fitzhugh border. The cup and saucer are a late nineteenth-century English version of the Chinese export service made for Martha Washington. A border of fifteen ovals encloses the names of the states of the Union.

6. Presidential China

Left, bottom: The purple-bordered, gold-trimmed Haviland china State Service ordered by President Lincoln was delivered in 1861. Lincoln demonstrated his respect for the early "buy American" legislation by having his imported china decorated with an appropriate American symbol, the eagle and shield.

Above: Following in the footsteps of his predecessors, Woodrow Wilson and Franklin D. Roosevelt, Harry S. Truman ordered his Presidential China from Lenox. This set was also used by Presidents Eisenhower and Kennedy.

Right, top and bottom: The French, one-thousand-piece Rutherford B. Hayes State Service was decorated, circa 1879, by Theodore Davis with illustrations of American flora and fauna. Mr. Davis's brightly colored service is typical of the flamboyant decorations so greatly admired by Victorian society.

Right, center: The Ulysses S. Grant State Service, made by Haviland & Company at Limoges, France, circa 1870, is decorated with the Coat-of-Arms of the United States and with sprays of native flowers.

The artistic developments and mechanical improvements of American glass are fully represented in their various regional aspects by the collection of pedigreed pieces shown at the Henry Ford Museum.

Left: The aquamarine, lily-pad-decorated sugar bowl was free blown at the Harrisburg Glass Works, New York, between 1841 and 1843.

Above, left: Frederick Mutzer was responsible for the sunburst-pattern, wisteria sugar bowl which was blown in a three-sectioned mold in New England, circa 1825.

Above, center: The unique, swirled, sixteen-ribbed deep amethyst covered sugar bowl was made by the Mantua Glass Works at Mantua, Ohio, circa 1822.

Above, right: This amethyst flask is from the eighteenth-century glasshouse of Frederick Amelung.

Below: Most of the lacy, pressed, and flint glass in the display case was manufactured by the Boston and Sandwich Glass Company and the New England Glass Company with the aid of a mechanical pressing machine during the second quarter of the nineteenth century.

Above, left: Colorful nineteenth-century whiskey bottles with historic or commemorative designs are one of the many special displays in the Museum's glass gallery.

Above, left: Typical of the ornate glass made to cater to American mid-Victorian taste is the blown honey-amber basket flecked with gold, 1860–1875.

Below, far left: Of special interest is the elegant cut and engraved tableware made in 1858 by his employees for Deming Jarves, founder of the Boston and Sandwich Glass Company.

Below: The purple-blue pressed glass syrup jar in the

Lincoln Drape pattern was manufactured at Pittsburgh, Pennsylvania, circa 1865.

Above: The unique collection of glassmaker's tools was used by Ralph Barber of Millville, New Jersey, in making his famed water lily paperweights, circa 1900.

Below: Louis Comfort Tiffany, the American glass master, signed the early twentieth-century three-handled blown vase with simulated antique patina.

II. Street of Shops
and the
Folk Art Collection

Above: Caleb Taft Blacksmith Shop.

The Street of Early American Shops represents hand-craftsmanship as it was practiced prior to the Industrial Revolution in America. The twenty-two shops are complete in architectural detail and are stocked with tools, merchandise, and accessories appropriate to their time and purpose. Cigar store Indians, shop figures, and other folk art are picturesque additions to the street. These shops, which were conceived by Edsel Ford, serve as a link between the more formal Decorative Arts Galleries and the Mechanical Arts Hall.

Above and below: Gurdlestone & Son, East India Merchants Shop.

Above and right: Gaily dressed nineteenth-century puppets in *Hadley's Toy Shop* share shelf space with pipsqueaks, pull toys, and carvings by the Pennsylvania-German woodcarvers Wilhelm Schimmel, Aaron Mounts, and John Reber.

Above: Corner Drug Store.

Above and below: Hadley's Toy Shop.

Far left, top: Mr. Morgan Hunting of Pine Plains, New York, painted by Ammi Phillips, New York, circa 1820.

Far left, bottom: Unidentified Child painted by William M. Prior, circa 1845, Boston, Massachusetts.

Near left: Cigar store Indian *Seneca John* carved and painted by Arnold and Peter Ruef, Tiffin, Ohio, circa 1880.

Right: Girl Coming Through Doorway, trompe l'oeil painting by George Washington Mark, Greenfield, Massachusetts, circa 1845.

Below: The Gettysburg Blues commanded by Colonel C. H. Buehler, Gettysburg, Pennsylvania, painted by an unidentified artist, circa 1845.

Using authentic early American tools and equipment housed in the Street of Shops, Museum and Village craftsmen demonstrate, at various times throughout the year, the arts of cabinetmaking, candlemaking, coopering, dyeing, glassblowing, pewter molding, pottery making, printing, quilting, rug hooking, shingle making, silk reeling, silversmithing, spinning, tinsmithing, tintyping, and weaving. The pewterer *(above, left)* molds spoons, plates, buttons, and miniature toys in the *David Cutler Pewter Shop (below). The* candlemaker *(above),* using beeswax and bayberry, fashions candles in a sixteen-tube metal and wood candle mold. Products from the craft shops are available to Museum visitors.

Above: (Left to right) Quart pewter tankard by William Will, Philadelphia, Pennsylvania, 1764–1798; pint pewter tankard by Frederick Bassett, New York, New York, 1761–1800; rare three-and-one-half pint pewter tankard by Francis Bassett I, New York City, 1715–1740.

Above: Tole document box from the New York–Vermont border area, circa 1825.

Right: Copper weathervane, circa 1875, found in Carlisle, Pennsylvania.

When merchandising their wares, shop owners often used signs painted with illustrations and lettering, or with three-dimensional representations of their products. The *A. Richardson Bootery* sign *(right)* employs both techniques. The interior of the shop *(below)* is stocked with shoes for men, women, and children. The nineteenth-century high-buttoned variety is complemented by a display case of silver and pearl-handled buttonhooks.

Woodcarvings like the dynamic New England poly-chrome and gilt eagle and serpent *(above)* were created in nineteenth-century shops similar to the *H. Card Turner and Carver Shop (below).*

No woman can resist the temptation to buy a smart hat. Jenny Lind, the world-famous nineteenth-century "Swedish Nightingale," probably purchased her basket-weave, ashwood bonnet *(left)* in a millinery shop filled with feminine accessories such as fans, buttons, hatpins, peacock feathers, and fancy ribbons. In the *Isabelle Bradley Millinery* establishment *(below)* there is also a collection of hatboxes covered with printed wallpaper which, during the nineteenth century, were called bandboxes.

The costume collection ranges from handmade eighteenth-century garments to early twentieth-century factory-produced articles. It provides an insight into the manners and customs of our ancestors. The brilliant yellow cotton petticoat *(near right)* is glazed and quilted, and was part of Deborah Read's trousseau when she married Benjamin Franklin in 1730. The child's cotton jacket *(far right)* is printed with portrait busts of George Washington. Coverlets, quilts, and other textiles are occasionally shown in special displays such as the *American Coverlets Exhibition (below)* which featured a loom on which jacquards were woven.

Sarah Furman Warner of Greenfield Hill, Connecticut, created an outstanding piece of needlework *(below)*. There is no record of the time consumed by her efforts, but through her precise and intricate design, her superb choice of fabrics for the appliqué, and her meticulous stitches, she created one of the greatest folk art masterpieces of all time.

The silk and cardboard sewing case *(near right)* from Doylestown, Pennsylvania, circa 1800, contains needles, thread, and other sewing equipment which might have been used to stitch the "Pine Tree" quilt *(bottom, center)*. The hand-woven wool, embroidered bedcover with blue wool fringe *(far right)* from New York State is initialed "S.M.B./A.L. 78." Square patterns of conventionalized motifs, embroidered in blue crewels, call to mind the decorative blue and white Delft tiles used around fireplaces in the Dutch-style homes of New Amsterdam.

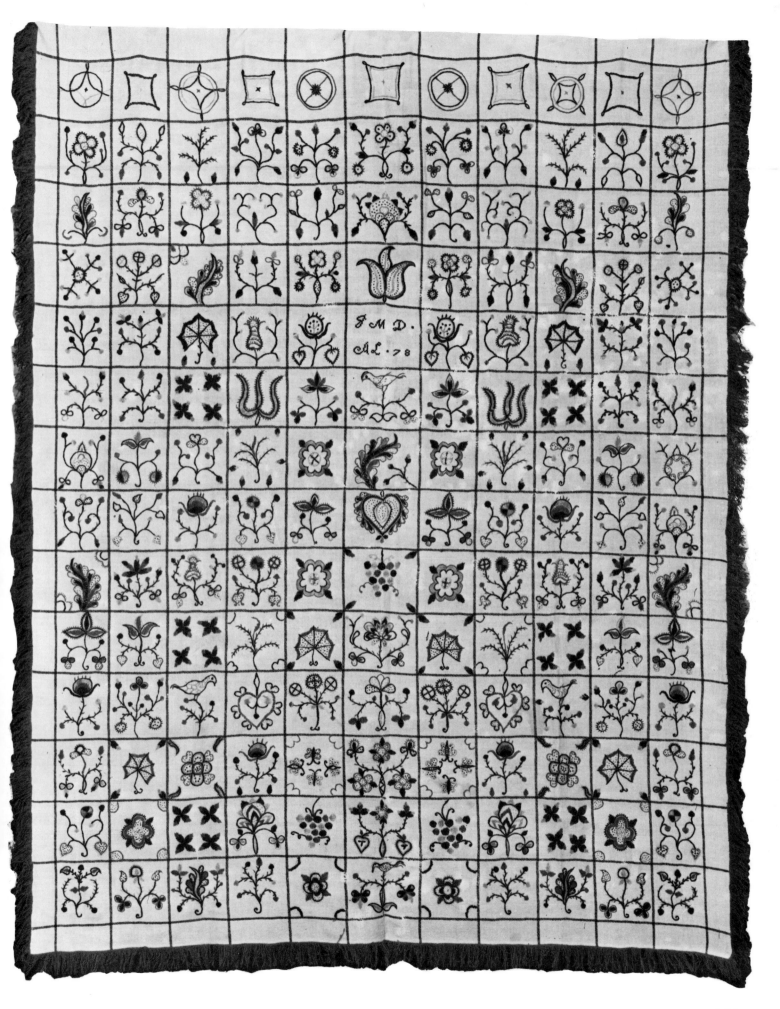

155

156

The age-old techniques of pottery-making are demonstrated by the Museum potter when he "throws" pots on a kick-wheel. Firing and glazing are completed in a large kiln in Greenfield Village's *Haggerty Power Plant*. The antique pottery collection displayed in the Street of Shops is comprised of several hundred American examples and includes outstanding pieces of redware and sgraffito (scratch-decorated pieces), as well as a large group of decorated gray stoneware. The winsome redware lion *(below)* was fashioned by John Bell (1826–1881) of Waynesboro, Pennsylvania. This Shenandoah Valley piece is covered with a bright yellow slip and its "coleslaw" mane is highlighted with a black glaze.

The foot-powered lathe under the rear window in the *Noyes Horn Comb Shop (left)* was employed for sawing and buffing the tortoiseshell used to create the elaborate combs in the window. A variety of small tools was necessary for the final piercing and carving.

Elegantly upholstered barber chairs were comforts provided in the more expensive nineteenth-century barbershops. The plush-upholstered walnut and iron example *(right)* was made in Rochester, New York, circa 1880, by the Archer Manufacturing Company. On the shelves of the *Charles Fowler Barber Shop (below)*, there is a gay collection of personalized shaving mugs.

The John F. Brown Gun and Locksmith Shop *(right)* contains a comprehensive collection of pistols, revolvers, muskets, rifles, shotguns, powderhorns, tomahawks, knives, and swords. Of special interest is a unique set of metal templates used by David Defibaugh, a gunsmith of Bedford County, Pennsylvania, circa 1835, to cut out brass inlay decorations for long rifles *(far right)*. The campaign chest and folding bed *(below)* were both used by General George Washington during the American Revolution. The bed was presented to him by General Peter Gansevoort of Schuylerville, New York. The chest was made in London, England, by William Chapple in 1783 and is fitted with cooking and eating utensils.

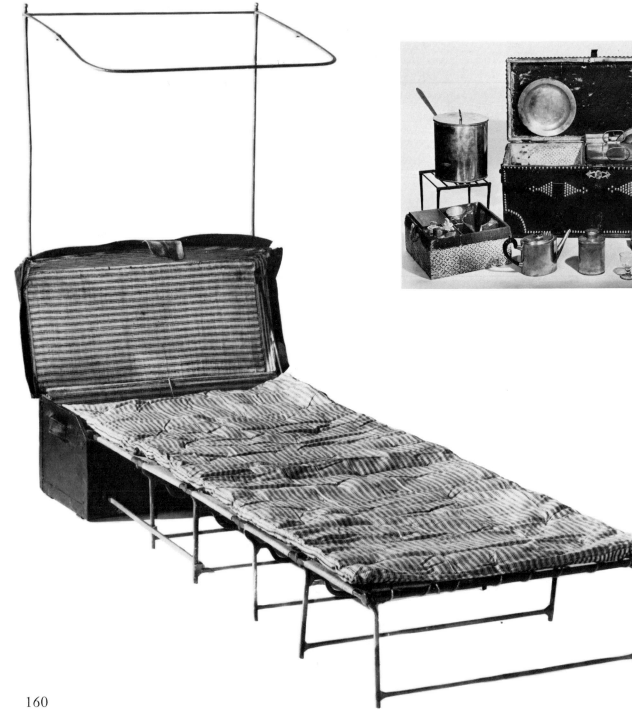

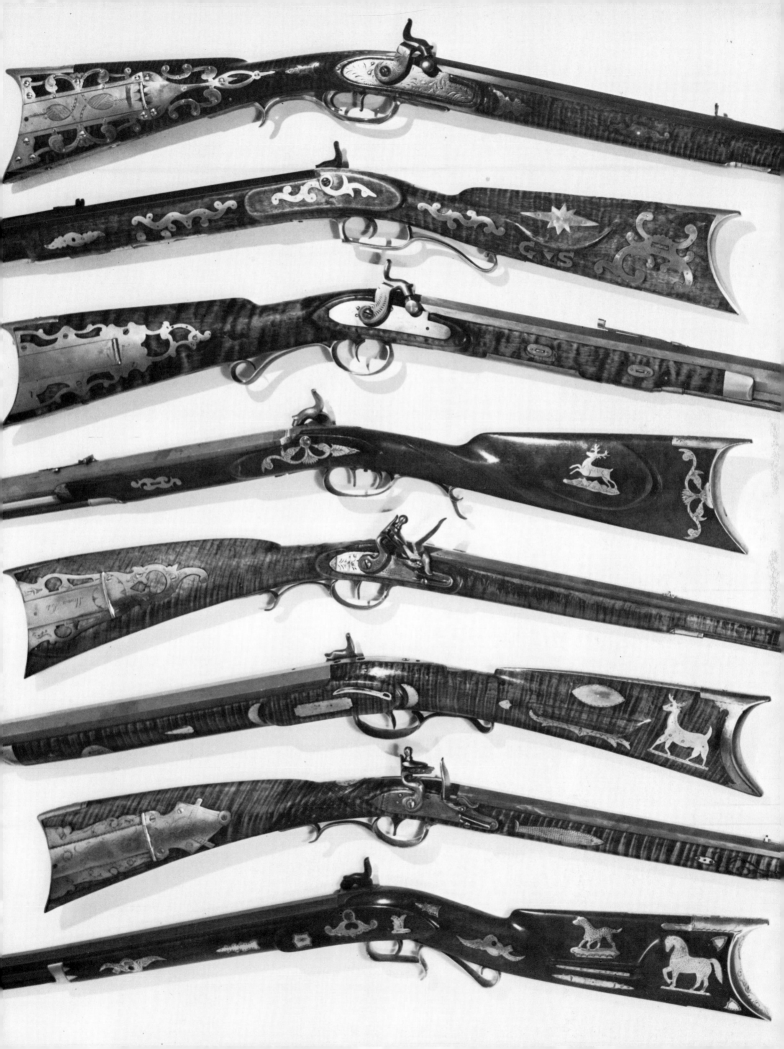

III. Mechanical Arts Hall

Within the vast eight-acre Mechanical Arts Hall of the Henry Ford Museum are represented the history of man's efforts at tilling the American soil and making it increasingly productive; the full story of man's utilization of increasingly complex tools, and of steam and electric power, to achieve consumer services and goods which far exceeded eighteenth- and even nineteenth-century credibility; of the development of illumination, from candlepower and whale oil to gas, the carbon arc, and electricity; of the full story of communication in its many forms: of the printing press, the linotype, and the typewriter, of the camera, the phonograph, the radio, and the television set, the telephone, the motion picture camera and projector. There are the full evidences of the growing household conveniences: the stove, the icebox and refrigerator, the sewing machine, the washing machine, the complex of kitchen tools. And, finally, there is represented the complete history of American transportation by boat, by horse-drawn vehicles, by bicycle and motorcycle, by train, by airplane, and by automobile.

Henry Ford had inscribed over the door of the original Ford Engineering Laboratory: "Mankind passes from the old to the new over a human bridge formed by those who labor in the three principal arts—agriculture, manufacturing, and transportation." He could, as well, have been referring to the story told by the collections at the Henry Ford Museum.

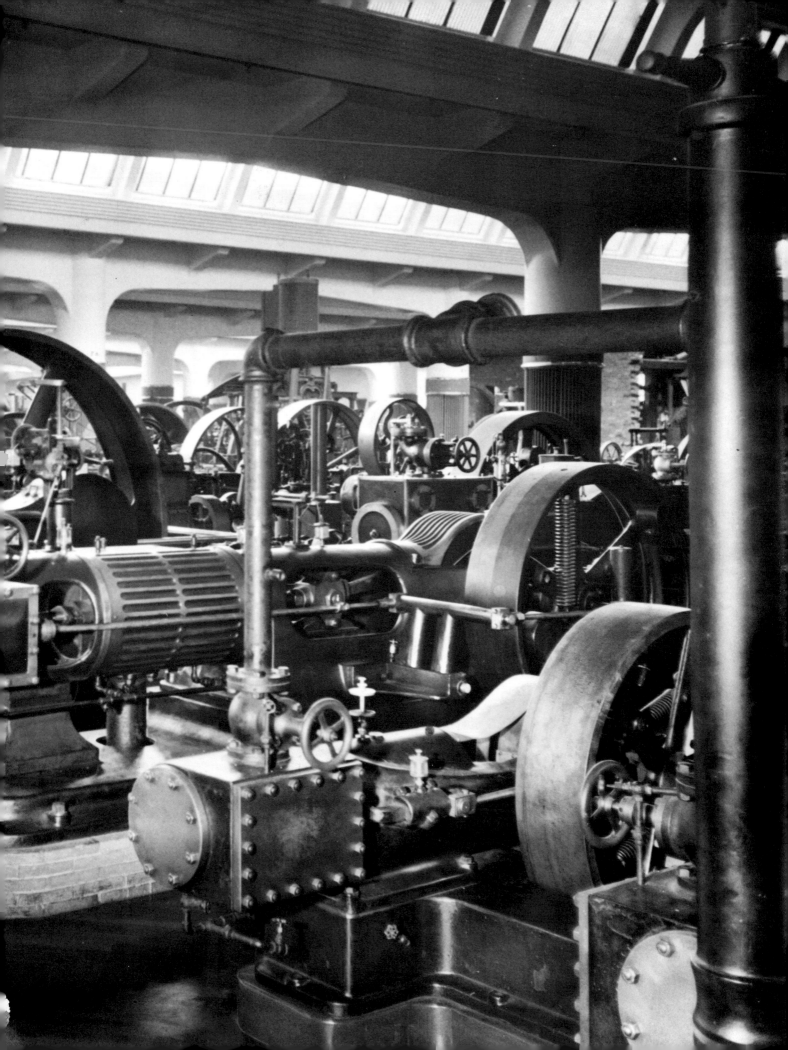

Henry Ford, who was born on a farm, regarded agriculture as one of the principal areas of American economic life which should be preserved in The Edison Institute. The agriculture collection which he began is one of the largest assemblages of farm implements and machines in the world. Collected widely in New England, the mid-Atlantic states, and the Middle West, these objects record some two hundred years of the evolving technology of American agriculture. They are grouped according to the farm activity in which they were used—plowing, seeding, cultivating, harvesting, and threshing grain—and according to the power sources used on farms. Tillage or cultivation involves loosening the soil to prepare and maintain a suitable seedbed for growing plants. The most important instrument of tillage is the plow. It developed from simple wooden handcrafted implements of English and Dutch origin into the factory-produced steel versions of the last one hundred years. Other tillage tools range from the hoe and spade to harrows, rollers, and cultivators.

Left, top: New England "strong plow" with a wooden moldboard sheathed in iron, eighteenth century, Biddeford, Maine.

Near left, top: Early cast iron moldboard plow, circa 1825, I. Tice, Hudson Furnace, Washington County, New York.

Near left, bottom: Chilled iron moldboard plow, late nineteenth century, Oliver Company, South Bend, Indiana.

Left, bottom: Spiked-tooth rotary harrow, circa 1865, Michigan.

Right, top: Grain and fertilizer drill, circa 1895, Superior Company, Springfield, Ohio.

Seeding was traditionally done by hand or with the aid of hand tools. During the nineteenth century, many "tinkerers" attempted to develop mechanical substitutes such as the grain drill for this task. These were later adapted to grass seeding and corn planting. Harvesting grain posed the most critical problem for the American farmer. The scarcity of labor and the short harvesting season determined how large a crop he could plant. Using the common grain harvesting tool of the eighteenth century—the sickle—one man could reap from one-half to three-quarters of an acre per day. The grain cradle increased this performance to about two acres. An extra man was required to bind the cut grain into sheaves and to stack them in shocks. The mechanical reaper, first developed in the 1830s by Cyrus H. McCormick and Obed Hussey, produced profound changes in this situation. Even these earliest reapers averaged from ten to twelve acres per day, with one man driving and one raking the cut grain. The later self-raking reaper of the 1860s eliminated one of these men, and the automatic binder, developed during the 1870s, ended the need for the four or more men binding after each machine.

Above: Grain cradle, mid-nineteenth century.

Right, top: Replica of Cyrus H. McCormick's 1834 patent reaper.

Below: Self-raking reaper, circa 1872, D. M. Osborn and Company, Auburn, New York.

1. Agriculture

Cereal grasses have always been among the most important American crops. Between harvesting and marketing, the crops must be threshed, separated, and cleaned. Two methods of threshing were used in early America—animal treading, in which the weight of the horses' hooves broke open the husk, and flailing, where frequent blows from a heavy wooden tool achieved the same result. The grain was separated by raking the stalks of the plant aside and shoveling the seed, mixed with the chaff and dirt, into a pile. This mixture was then poured from a winnowing basket or "fan," allowing the wind to carry away the lighter impurities while the heavier grain fell to the ground. Fanning mills, introduced early in the nineteenth century, improved this process by using an artificial blast of air and sifting screens of varying sizes. After the development of the mechanical threshing machine later in the nineteenth century, these three operations were combined.

Right, bottom: Fanning mill, M. Elliot's patent, 1831, Massachusetts.

Below: Threshing machine, circa 1850, Watertown Agricultural Works, Watertown, New York.

Above: Steam threshing scene from an 1884 catalogue of J. I. Case Company, Racine, Wisconsin.

Below: Flail and winnowing basket, mid-nineteenth century.

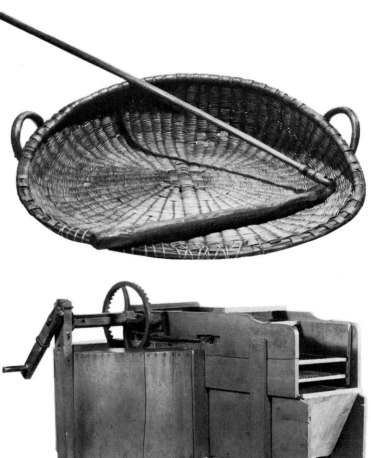

The mechanization of American agriculture—particularly of threshing—pointed up the need for new sources of power to replace the traditional horse and ox. During the nineteenth century, steam was universally thought to be the answer. In 1849, small portable steam engines, built specifically to power threshing machines, became available. In order to replace the horse completely, a "steam plow," or self-propelled steam traction engine, was necessary. It was not until the 1870s that the first reliable traction engines came into use. Because of their size, extreme weight, and cost, these engines were practicable only on larger farms, particularly in the West. It was the lightweight gasoline tractor of the twentieth century which finally supplied the long-sought power needs of the average American farmer.

Above: Portable steam engine, circa 1878, Fishkill Landing Machine Company, Fishkill, New York.

Right: Collection of ponderous traction and portable steam engines on exhibit in the Henry Ford Museum.

Below: Henry Ford demonstrating his earliest tractor, an experimental model of 1907–1908.

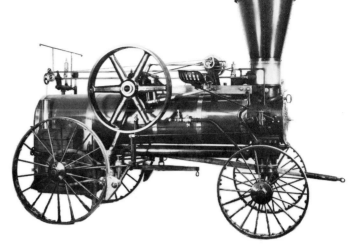

Today, in the era of liberated women, many of whom work outside the home, housework is fitted into and around other schedules. Before the days of packaged foods, wrinkle-free fabrics, and automatic appliances, housework was done on a rigorously followed schedule: Monday, washing; Tuesday, ironing; Wednesday, sewing; Thursday, shopping; Friday, cleaning; and Saturday, baking.

The domestic arts collections in the Henry Ford Museum illustrate the changes in American homemaking techniques from the seventeenth through the early twentieth century. These collections demonstrate the progress in homemaking from hearth cookery and handmade implements to the present age of mechanization.

During the middle and late nineteenth century, improved technology produced appliances such as the 1867 Singer Sewing Machine *(left, center)*, made in New York, and the Jewel Coal-Saving Range *(far left, top)* of the 1880s to lighten the homemaker's job. And rather than use a washtub for the laundry, she could now use one of the many washing machines, such as the Boss Washing Machine *(below)*, patented in 1888.

Although she probably still used handmade wooden bowls *(left, bottom)*, she now had her choice of factory-made kitchen implements.

Hand-decorated mass-produced tin kitchens *(right)* were used for storing flour, coffee, and spices safely. Tin pastry boards with a built-in shelf for storing the accompanying rolling pin were also available.

2. Domestic Arts

The story of civilization has recorded many attempts to develop improved methods of artificial illumination. Until man mastered artificial lighting, his activities were confined to the daylight hours.

In 1879 Thomas Edison made electric light a practicality. Henry Ford greatly admired Edison's contribution and honored him by forming a lighting collection to illustrate the development of lighting in the United States from the period of household improvisation to that of industrialization.

During the period of America's first settlement, candles, rushlights, and grease lamps were the prime sources of artificial light. Aside from those few articles which were imported, each household was responsible for creating its own lighting implements. Wrought iron rush holders from the seventeenth century *(near right and bottom left)* were commonly brought to America from England and the Continent.

When craft shops developed, the manufacture of lighting devices moved from the home to professional workers in iron, tin, and pottery. Blacksmiths, like Peter Derr, Berks County, Pennsylvania, made lamps. Derr's brass, copper, and iron betty *(above center)* is dated 1848. Betty lamps were also mounted on stands and were adjustable *(center)* like this Ohio example.

American potters like S. Routson from Ohio, working in the 1840s, contributed to the development of lighting devices by making pottery grease lamps *(right, center)*.

Among lighting devices of European origin are the water refractors *(right)* used by lacemakers, cobblers, and watchmakers to intensify candlelight. These ingenious devices were the forerunners of the later bull's-eye lamps. A woodcut *(right, top)* from John White's *Art Treasury,* 1688, illustrates how these devices were used.

172

Lard and lard oil lamps were indigenous to the United States. During the second quarter of the nineteenth century inventors, in their search for a substitute for costly whale oil, turned to lard as a lamp fuel.

The hanging tin and brass lard oil solar lamp *(upper left)* was manufactured by Cornelius & Co., Philadelphia, and is based upon Robert Cornelius's patent of April 18, 1843. The pewter chandelier *(lower left),* made by William S. Lawrence of Meriden, Connecticut, has three decorated pewter fish fonts mounted around his patented 1834 lard burner. The tin lamp *(above left)* was patented by Zuriel Swope on March 13, 1860, in Lancaster, Pennsylvania. Tilton & Sleeper, Freemont, New Hampshire, manufactured the tin lamp *(above right)* using the I. Smith and J. Stonesifer patent granted August 8, 1854, in Boonsboro, Maryland.

Although lard lamps came into common use, whale oil was not totally displaced. Among the very rare patented whale oil lighting devices is the railroad conductor's lantern *(right),* patented by Philos Blake on January 13, 1852, in New Haven, Connecticut, and manufactured by D. D. Miller in New York.

American artifacts comprise the bulk of the Henry Ford Museum's lighting collection *(below)*, but lighting devices from ancient civilizations and foreign countries are also represented.

Many fine examples of political parade torches are included. The gilded sheet copper, eagle-shaped torch *(left)* was used for campaigns during the 1860s.

An outstanding example of the Boston and Sandwich Glass Company's production is an overlay glass lamp fitted with a double kerosene burner *(right)*. This lamp dates from about 1875, and is one of the tallest of its kind.

The gilded wood and gesso electric chandelier *(opposite)* was designed for and used in "Fair Lane," Henry Ford's Dearborn home, which he and Mrs. Ford first occupied in 1915.

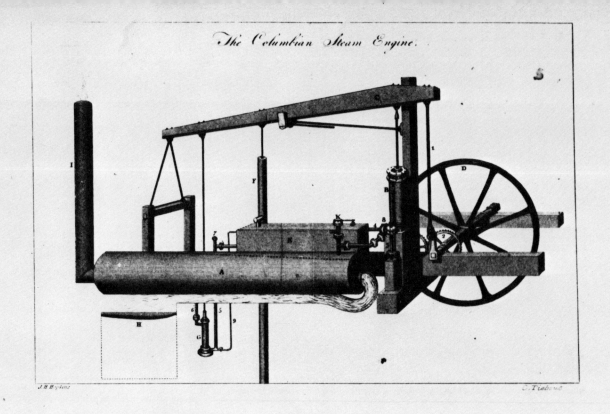

The Columbian Steam Engine.

LICENSE.

KNOW all Men by these presents, That I, Oliver Evans, Steam-Engineer, of the city of Philadelphia. have received of ~~The Marrietta Steam Mill C?~~ of ~~the state of Ohio~~ county. state of ~~Ohio~~ ——— the sum of *Four Hundred & eighty Dollars* ——— in full payment for a Steam-Engine, and for License hereby granted to the said *Marrietta Steam Mill C?* their heirs, executors, administrators and assigns, to use one of my patented Steam-Engines, constructed on the principle of retaining the steam in strong boilers, in order to increase the heat, and thereby increase the elastic power of the steam until *they* obtain the power of *Twenty* ——— horses to be exerted by *their* engine: The power of a horse to be rated at 150 pounds raised perpendicularly 220 feet per minute,—or the piston of the engine to describe 7920 cubic inches of space per minute, (for each horse power) carrying an average load of 50 pounds to each superficial square inch of the area of its end; according to the rules laid down for ascertaining the power of my steam-engine, in my book entitled " The Abortion of the Young Steam-Engineer's Guide," and to apply and use the same *in Marrietta State of Ohio to the grinding of grain or to any other purposes whatever* ———

——— '' ——— '' ———

for and during my present or any future patent term. Witness my hand and seal this *Tenth* ——— day of *November 1812*

Witness present

Leonard Folwison
James M'Culloch
Stackhouse & Rogers

Oliver Evans
Geo: Evans patent a
For Oliver Evans

4. Power

The Industrial Revolution, which created modern society and civilization, began with the development of the steam engine. One of the world's largest and most complete collections of steam engines, showing the development of this prime mover from its beginnings at the hand of Thomas Newcomen (1663–1729) in the eighteenth century to modern times, is at the Henry Ford Museum. The oldest complete atmospheric steam engine in the collection, and perhaps in the world *(right)*, came from the Chambers Colliery near Ashton-under-Lyne in Lancashire, England, where it was used to pump water from a mine beginning about 1760.

The second major development of the steam engine was undertaken by James Watt (1736–1819) between the years 1765 and 1788. He doubled engine efficiency by adding a separate condenser and by using the steam to push the piston from either side. He also added a governor which helped to maintain a steady speed, and developed innovations which changed the movement of the atmospheric engine from a to-and-fro motion to a rotary motion. These alterations made the engine more adaptable to factory work. An exact duplicate of Watt's famous Sun-and-Planet engine of

1788 *(below)* incorporates all these improvements. There are other original Watt-type engines on display.

Watt believed that only low pressure should be used in a steam engine; however, high pressure was to be the direction of future development. Oliver Evans (1755–1819) was one of the first Americans to build high-pressure engines. He issued a license *(left)* on November 10, 1812, to the "Mariatta Steam Mill Company" at Marietta, Ohio, for the operation of a twenty-horsepower reciprocating beam engine which he sold to the firm for "grinding of grain or to any other purposes whatever. . . ."

Despite the fact that the Watt engines were more efficient than the earlier atmospheric engines, the latter continued to be built for several decades after Watt and his business partner, Matthew Boulton, began selling theirs in 1774. The late atmospheric engine and engine house *(below)* were probably built around 1800 and were used for pumping water at Windmill End Station, Netherton, Dudley, Worcestershire, England, until 1928. It is interesting to note that the engine has both a crank and a separate condenser. The small English engine *(left, top)*, from the Howe Dye Works in England, was used from the time of its construction in 1830 until a century later. The well-known nineteenth-century American engine *(left, middle)* built by C. H. Brown at Fitchburg, Massachusetts, in 1881, was popular because of its high efficiency and reliability.

By the end of the nineteenth century, the steam engine, at least in many smaller installations, was supplanted by a newcomer—the internal combustion engine *(right)*. The taller engine, with a capacity of approximately two horsepower, was made about 1875 by the English firm of Crossley Brothers under the 1867 English patents of Nicholas Otto and Eugene Langen. Although this early Otto and Langen engine was quite noisy and at times vibrated considerably, it was widely used until replaced by their four-stroke engine of 1878. The shorter engine with a capacity of about one-half horsepower, built about a decade later by the English firm of J. E. H. Andrew, Stockport, England, under the 1872 and 1875 patents of A. deBisschop, was dependable and simple to operate.

Though ancient Greece has long been considered the cradle of the fine arts, that civilization also made many contributions to the field of practical technology. One of its most important developments was the lathe. The wooden lathe of antiquity did not begin to change in design until the end of the eighteenth century, when iron and steel were used for its construction. The pole lathe *(above)*, constructed by a nineteenth-century American woodworker, is similar in many ways to its Greek prototype.

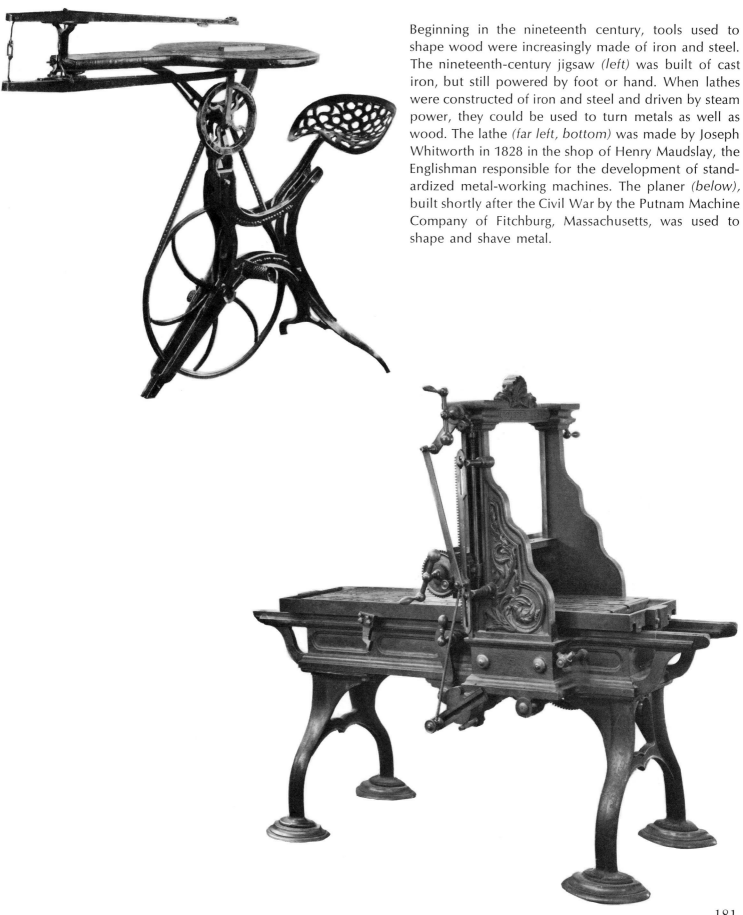

Beginning in the nineteenth century, tools used to shape wood were increasingly made of iron and steel. The nineteenth-century jigsaw *(left)* was built of cast iron, but still powered by foot or hand. When lathes were constructed of iron and steel and driven by steam power, they could be used to turn metals as well as wood. The lathe *(far left, bottom)* was made by Joseph Whitworth in 1828 in the shop of Henry Maudslay, the Englishman responsible for the development of standardized metal-working machines. The planer *(below)*, built shortly after the Civil War by the Putnam Machine Company of Fitchburg, Massachusetts, was used to shape and shave metal.

Great advances in communications—photography, telegraphy, printing—and in the field of applied electricity were realized in the nineteenth century. One of the earliest practical methods of photography was developed by the Frenchman, Louis J. M. Daguerre, in 1839. His process, which spread rapidly throughout the world, was brought to America by inventor Samuel F. B. Morse. The wooden camera and tripod *(left)*, constructed about 1845, is one of the earliest complete Daguerrean outfits known. The 1889 Edison camera marked the transition from still photography to motion pictures. The model *(below)* was probably made in 1896 for the Mutoscope patent trials, where it was used to prove Edison's prior involvement with the practical development of the motion picture.

The process of printing was improved in a number of ways during the nineteenth century. From the days of Gutenberg in the mid-1400s, most printing presses had been constructed of wood and utilized a large screw to apply pressure to the type and paper. In 1813, Edward Bevan, an Englishman, introduced the Columbian press. It was an all-iron machine in which the speed of printing was increased by replacing the screw with a variation of a toggle joint. The Columbian press was further improved in 1821 by Samuel Rust, inventor of the Washington press *(left, below)*. This example, made by the famous R. Hoe Company of New York City, contributed much to American history. Sometime in the late 1840s it was purchased by "Judge" J. Judson Ames of Baton Rouge, Louisiana, who printed the newspaper that helped elect Zachary Taylor to the presidency in 1848. Like so many Americans in 1849, Ames went to California in search of gold. There he sold the press to Major E. Sherman, who, during the early years of the Civil War, advocated the Union cause so strongly in his journal that he was forced to protect his press with an armed guard. Sherman moved to Aurora, Nevada, where he founded the *Esmeralda Star* in 1862. It was at that time that the young Mark Twain used this press.

The invention of the typewriter made a large contribution toward the economic independence of women in the nineteenth century. The 1874 model *(right, below)*, manufactured by the Remington Arms Company under the Sholes-Glidden patent of 1868, is one of the earliest mass-produced, commercially-practical typewriters.

Advances in printing occurred through the mechanization of the type-composing process. The keyboard-composing machine *(above)*, an early form of linotype machine, was devised in 1891 by H. Lee and E. LeBrun. It made a matrix in which the text for an entire page could be cast.

The small telegraph set *(left, bottom)*, manufactured by Hugo Gernsback, one of the foremost pioneers in the development of the commercial wireless, was marketed in the form of a "do-it-yourself" kit in 1906. It was the first production wireless telegraph in the world to be advertised for sale. Many of the electrical experimenters of the day obtained their initial experience with what was later to be termed "radio" from a gadget like this.

The phonograph helped inaugurate the American home entertainment industry. One of the more elegant versions *(right)* was made about 1910 following the Edison patents of February 1878. It is interesting to note that Edison, almost from the beginning, attempted to enhance his motion picture system by synchronizing it with recorded sound.

Until the twentieth century, the application of electricity to the needs of mankind was a very slow process. In the last quarter of the eighteenth century, electrostatic machines *(above),* similar to this one made by I. M. Wightman in Boston, Massachusetts, were fashioned. The device replaced the primitive method of making electric sparks by rubbing glass and animal fur together. More than a century elapsed before generators for electric lighting were developed.

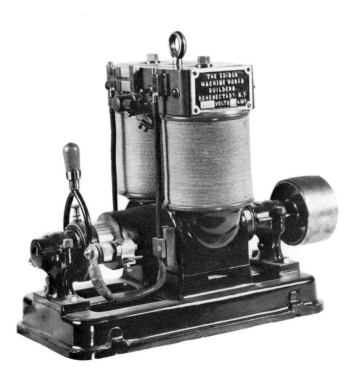

Thomas Alva Edison, who perfected a direct current system between 1878 and 1882, was the first to devise a practical, commercial method of illuminating the home with incandescent light from a central power station. The steamship *Columbia,* voyaging from New York around Cape Horn to Portland, Oregon, was equipped with one of Edison's earliest commercial incandescent lamp installations powered by the Edison bipolar generator *(right),* which was dubbed the "Long-legged Mary Ann." The more familiar 1882 Edison generator *(far left, bottom),* designed and constructed at the Edison Machine Works at Schenectady, New York, soon replaced the 1880 "Mary Ann."

Because of economic considerations, the Edison direct current system was limited in its transmission of power to distances of a mile or less. During the early 1890s, the alternating current systems of Westinghouse and General Electric superseded it. The Westinghouse meter *(near left, bottom),* devised by Shallenberger in 1888, measured this relatively new form of current. The General Electric rotary converter *(below),* which appeared in the early 1890s, was a combination AC motor–DC generator device that transformed alternating current to direct current. It gave the alternating system all the advantages of direct current with little power loss during transmission.

The nineteenth and twentieth centuries saw a steady increase in the exploitation of electricity for the field of communications—the telegraph of the 1830s, the telephone of the 1870s, radio of the 1890s, and television of the 1920s. In the Museum installation (bottom) are two of the more important advances in wire communications—Edison's quadruplex telegraph of 1874, which enabled four messages to be sent simultaneously over the same wire, and the step-by-step system telephone switchboard, introduced on a large scale about 1920. The wall magneto telephone (right), although used until relatively recently, dates from the mid-1880s.

Radio broadcasts to the general public began around 1920. The early RCA Radiola (below), manufactured about 1924, was one of the more popular receivers. Headphones were necessary, since the set was not powerful enough to drive a loudspeaker.

Attempts made during the nineteenth century to transmit pictures by telegraph were not especially successful. Once radio broadcasting became popular, inventors attempted to devise ways to transmit pictures by wireless or, as we know it, television. C. Francis Jenkins, a motion picture apparatus inventor of Washington, D.C., developed in 1923 the optical scanner (far right). This device was used to create signals that could be converted to electrical impulses which then could be transmitted by wireless.

7. Transportation

The story of America is the story of transportation. It is portrayed in the Henry Ford Museum by the world's largest collection of airplanes, automobiles, bicycles, boats, carriages, locomotives, motorcycles, sleighs, streetcars, trucks, and wagons.

Explorers and adventurers came to the shores of America in wooden sailing ships. By the eighteenth century, colonists in some areas had not only occupied the seacoast, but penetrated inland as far as navigable waters would permit. Horses and horse-drawn wagons provided transportation for settlers as they pushed ever westward over old Indian trails. Freight was transported in the Conestoga wagon, a distinctively American vehicle developed to meet the peculiar requirements of the terrain. A large network of canals built during the 1820s to extend the navigable waters furthered the settlement and development of western lands. Horse- or mule-drawn barges traveled the new waterways conveying both freight and passengers. With the passage of another decade, the steam locomotive and the railroad train, initially developed in England, were introduced into America. For the first time in the history of man, speed far in excess of animal power could be attained and areas impossible to reach by canals could be exploited. More reliable water transportation was offered by ships using the steam engine as a source of power.

New modes of personal transportation developed also, although in rural areas the farmer still depended on the horse and buggy. Private transportation for the average urbanite was limited to foot travel until the introduction of the English high-wheel bicycle in 1880. Gradually horse-drawn streetcars of the 1880s were replaced by the far speedier, electric-powered streetcars in the 1890s, which provided convenient public transportation.

Although the automobile had its inception earlier in Europe, it was rapidly developed in America at the turn of the century as a new form of personal transportation for the common man. Henry Ford, one of several early automotive experimenters, was the first to perfect an entirely reliable and sturdy low-priced vehicle. His Model T, introduced in 1909, literally put the world on wheels. Ford's innovation in 1913 of the moving assembly line revolutionized automobile manufacturing and ultimately all manufacturing methods.

The airplane is a truly American invention, starting with the first heavier-than-air flight by the Wright brothers in 1903. It was a full decade after that flight, however, before World War I spurred intensive interest in and technical development of the flying machine. Charles A. Lindbergh's solo flight in a single-engine plane from New York to Paris in 1927 dramatically demonstrated to the world that the airplane was a rapid, reliable, and safe means of transportation. William T. Piper's "Cub" went a long way toward putting America on wings, just as Henry Ford's "Flivver" had put America on wheels.

The Association of Licensed Automobile Manufacturers purchased from George Selden his 1895 patent for a "forecarriage." In 1903 the Association, which operated as a monopoly to control the construction of automobiles, sued Henry Ford for infringement of the Selden patent. This car, built by Selden in 1907, proved to the court that his patent was workable. However, the patent was declared valid only for two-cycle engines and the court held that Henry Ford's four-cycle engine did not constitute an infringement. The suit was dismissed and Mr. Ford thus became known as the "trust buster." The dismissal ultimately freed the whole automobile industry from the burden of paying royalties to the ALAM.

The first production Ford, this 1903 Model A Runabout, firmly established the permanence of the Ford Motor Company.

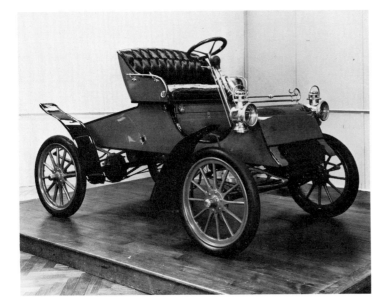

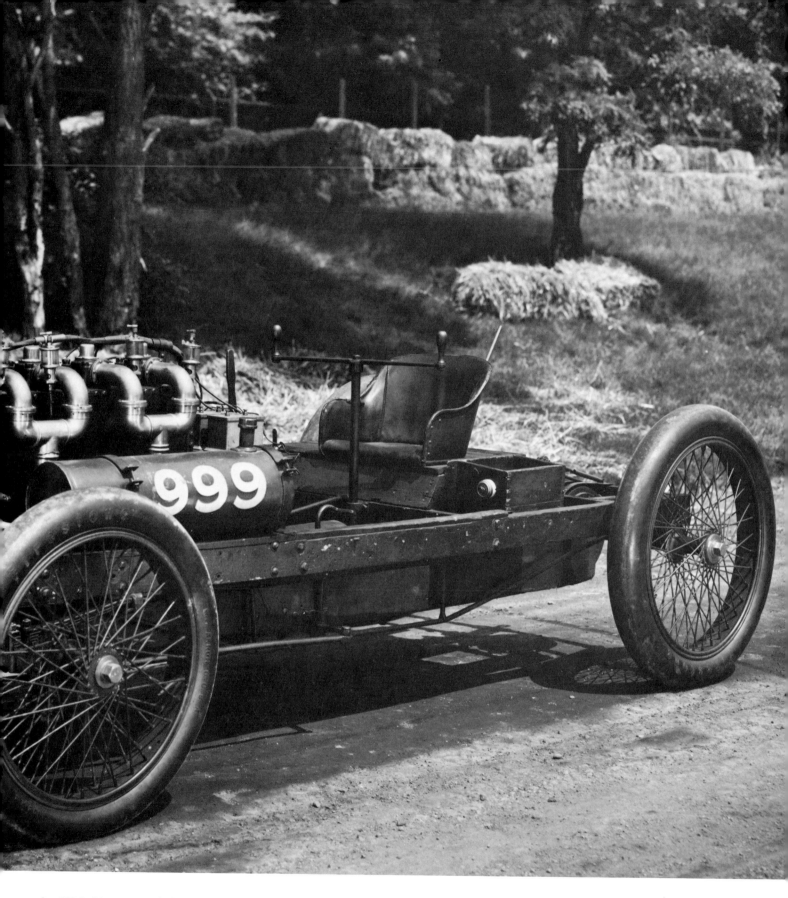

In 1902, Henry Ford designed and built this pioneer racer, dubbed "999," after a fast New York Central locomotive. Driven by Barney Oldfield, "999" became world-famous as a consistent race winner and record breaker. In 1904, Henry Ford personally drove "999" on the ice of Lake St. Clair to set a one-mile record at 91.4 miles per hour. The "999" engine has an impressive 1157-cubic-inch displacement.

Cadillac Runabout, 1903
One-cylinder, chain-driven automobile produced by Henry Leland.

Thomas Flyer Touring, 1906
A similar Flyer, in 1908, won the daring "Race Around the World" from New York to Paris via California and Asia.

Holsman Auto Buggy, 1903
A motorized buggy with tiller steering and a "rope" drive on pulleys.

Sears Motor Buggy, 1909
In 1909 the mail-order house of Sears, Roebuck & Company offered the Sears Motor Buggy at a cost of $325.

Martini Touring, 1903
Swiss-made with vertical radiator, four-cylinder engine, clutch, transmission, and shaft drive.

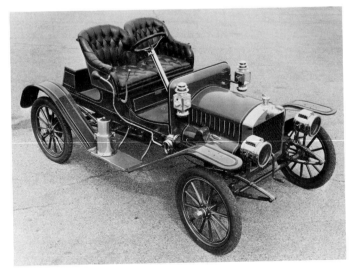

Maxwell-Briscoe Junior Runabout, 1911
Featured all-metal bodies, multiple cylinders, and shaft drive.

Above: Henry Ford introduced his famous 1909 Model T as the "Universal Car—rugged, dependable, simple, and low in cost so that nearly everybody can own one." Anxious to prove this claim, Henry Ford entered two cars in the Guggenheim transcontinental endurance race in 1909. The Model T Ford Racer No. 2 came in first in the New York-to-Seattle run, winning out over bigger, heavier, more powerful, and more costly cars. Based on this success, more than fifteen million Model T Fords were ultimately built.

Below: Electric automobiles such as the 1914 Detroit Electric Coupe, personal car of Mrs. Henry Ford, were greatly favored by the ladies, who desired simple, clean, quiet, slow, and sedate personal transportation. The very heavy lead–sulfuric acid batteries, contained in the fore and aft compartments, restricted use of electric cars to paved streets and to short runs of about thirty miles between battery charges. The basic limitations of electric automobiles have still not been overcome despite technological advances.

Above: The famous Rolls-Royce Silver Ghost model, so named for its smooth, quiet-running qualities, was introduced in 1907. Four specially prepared Silver Ghost models, dubbed "Alpine Eagles," were entered as a factory team in the 1913 Austrian Alpine Trials and figuratively flew over the difficult 1,645-mile mountain racecourse to win seven prizes, scoring brilliantly against much larger cars. A single "Eagle," entered by an individual, set a nonstop record in the 1914 Alpine Trials.

Left, center: The five-passenger Ford Model T sedan was fitted with an electric starter and demountable rims in 1919. Thereafter, ladies could drive the Model T without having to crank the engine, and flat tires could easily be changed. This sedan body, first introduced in 1915, was so popular that by 1925 closed cars outsold open-bodied cars in America.

Left, bottom: Edsel Ford received this 1916 Mercer as a wedding gift. Despite the touring body design, Mercer was a real sports car of its day. "Stock" Mercer runabouts were driven to many victories by such famous drivers as Ralph DePalma, Barney Oldfield, and Billy Knipper.

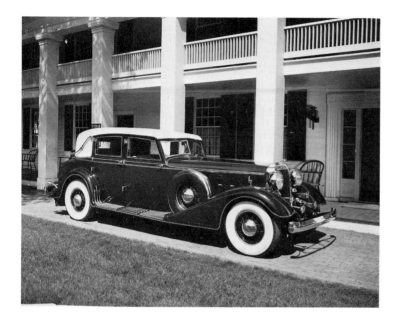

Left: This Chrysler Custom Imperial Landau, appropriate for either chauffeur or owner driving, was designed and built in 1932 especially for Walter P. Chrysler's personal use. In addition to its special aluminum body and high-compression engine, this classic car has many distinctive interior appointments including desk, bar, vanity cases, speedometer, and clock in the rear compartment.

Bottom: This Model A Ford Number One, built on October 21, 1927, with a Tudor body, was personally test driven by Henry Ford before receiving his approval for mass production. It was subsequently fitted with its present Phaeton body, trimmed in leather, and presented to Thomas A. Edison. The Model A, new for 1928, was not a revamped Model T, but so completely original that Henry Ford said, "We are wiping the slate clean and starting all over again with Model A." It is shown parked in front of Edison's Florida *Fort Myers Laboratory,* now at Greenfield Village.

The British Rolls-Royce was established as a marque of excellence and opulence by its 1907 Silver Ghost model. In 1926 the six-cylinder Phantom I was introduced. The great American financier, J. P. Morgan, had a limousine body *(above)* custom built by the well-known Brewster & Company of New York and fitted to a 1926 Phantom chassis.

Stutz, famous for "the car that made good in a day," produced between 1911 and 1934 a long line of illustrious champions of road and racecourse. The aptly named Bearcat sports model *(upper right)*, built in 1923, was powered by a four-cylinder, "T" head, dual-ignition engine. Each Bearcat, a glamorous symbol of the flapper-flask-and-raccoon-coat era, was individually tested for performance and speed on the Indianapolis Speedway, scene of its initial successes, before being delivered to the customer.

The 1955 Mercedes 300 SLR race car *(right)*, winner of the 1955 World Championship for Sports Cars, was the last of the great competition models built by Daimler-Benz, A.G., at Stuttgart, Germany. Its eight-cylinder engine, with double overhead camshafts, developed 295 horsepower with a displacement of only 180 cubic inches and drove the car to a speed of 180 miles per hour. The Daimler-Benz racing team was retired from competition when the 300 SLR had proved its excellence beyond doubt.

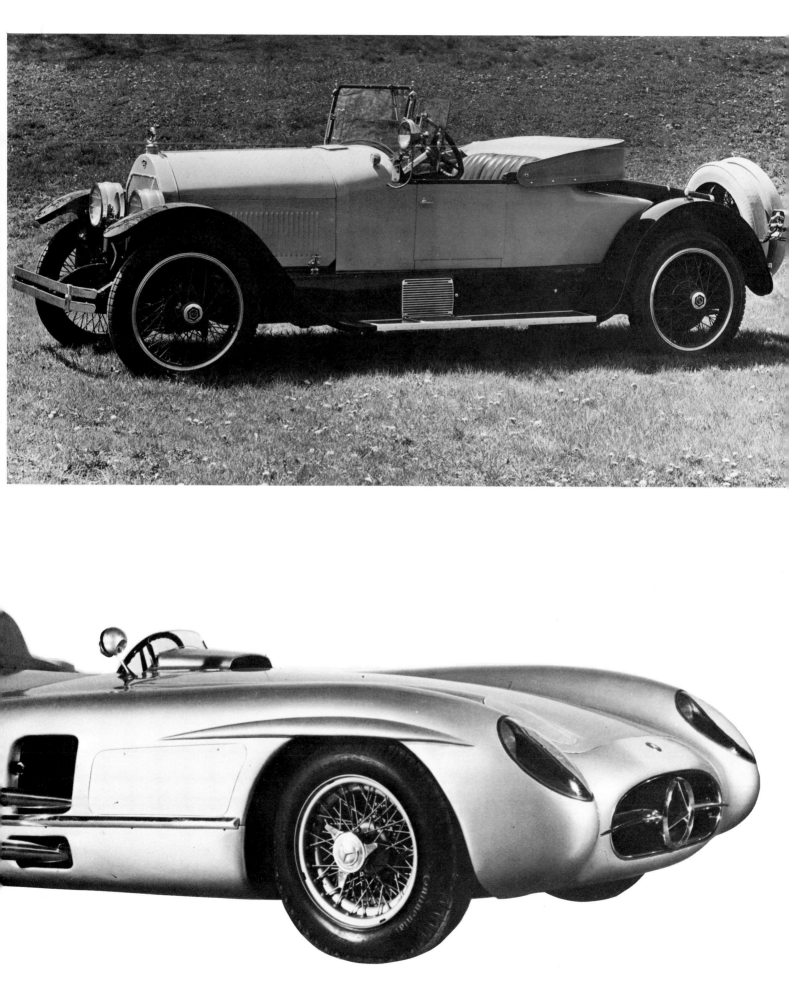

The specially constructed Lincoln limousine (above) prepared for President Franklin D. Roosevelt in 1939, was dubbed the "Sunshine Special" because he often rode in it with the top folded down. In 1942, it was returned to the factory and equipped with armor plate and bullet-proof glass, tires, and gas tank for a total weight of nearly five tons. The car was used by President Roosevelt during his historic conferences at Yalta, Casablanca, Teheran, and Malta, and by President Truman until 1950.

This 1940 Crown Imperial Chrysler, specially built and fitted with a handmade Derham body, was used for nearly twenty years in New York City's fabulous official parades and receptions. Its passenger list is a veritable roll-call of the world's dignitaries—kings, ambassadors, statesmen, and notable personages in war, peace, the arts, and the sciences. In the photograph (right), General Dwight D. Eisenhower responds to the excitement of a "ticker-tape parade."

The massive, specially-built 1950 Lincoln convertible was the official car for four Presidents of the United States. It was first used by President Truman *(below)*, then by President Eisenhower who had the plastic "bubble top" *(bottom)* fitted over the tonneau. Presidents Kennedy *(left, bottom)* and Johnson occasionally used it as a second car until its retirement in 1967.

Increase of automobile traffic made necessary the development of traffic signals. In October of 1920, the world's first three-color, four-direction, electrically operated signal *(right)*, designed by Superintendent W. L. Potts of the Detroit Police Department Signal Bureau, was installed at the intersection of Woodward Avenue and Fort Street in Detroit, Michigan. S. W. Raymond built the Conoco gasoline station *(below)*, in 1915 and installed it at Adrian, Michigan. For the first time, the purchaser was able to see from the gauge the exact amount of fuel being delivered into his vehicle. It was the first visible gasoline dispensing station in the United States. Several hundred of these stations were ultimately built of steel and sold commercially.

The Museum collections include a vast array of accessories demonstrating the artistry and craftsmanship lavished on many early automobiles. The brass snakehead *(above)*, perhaps the most famous bulb horn ever made, was crafted by the English firm of S. Smith & Sons, circa 1910. Self-generating gas headlamps were used on many cars in the early twentieth century. The brass model *(right)* was made circa 1907. The magnificent crystal radiator ornament *(center)*, manufactured around 1925, and titled "Spirit of the Wind," is one of the finest produced at the Lalique Cristallerie in France. Proud owners often installed a special light at the base of these ornaments to highlight the sculpture.

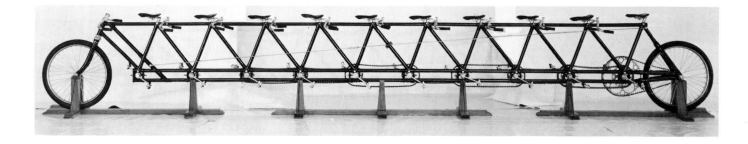

The high-wheel bicycle, transplanted from England to America about 1880, sprang to immediate popularity as a means of personal transportation. Clubs, such as the League of American Wheelmen, promoted improved roads, road signs, and "tourism."

The Columbia high-wheel, or "ordinary," bicycle *(left)* was built in Boston in 1888 by the Pope Manufacturing Company. The size of the large wheel, limited only by the length of a man's legs, determined speed; the small wheel provided a modicum of stability. Pope Manufacturing Company also pioneered in the manufacture of automobiles after 1900.

The ten-man bicycle, "Oriten" *(above),* is one of the largest in the world. It was built in 1896 as an advertising novelty by the Waltham Manufacturing Company, makers of the famous Orient safety bicycles. Successor to the "ordinary" bicycle, which often pitched its rider over the handlebar onto his head, the safety bicycle had wheels of equal size, pneumatic tires, and chain-and-sprocket drive for speed. Among the most popular was the Rambler *(right)* built in 1892 in Chicago, Illinois, by Gormully & Jeffery Manufacturing Company, inventors of the clincher pneumatic tire. Jeffery began building the Rambler automobile in 1902.

The popularity of motorcycles reached its height shortly after World War I. The 1919 Excelsior 45-cubic inch, twin-cylinder motorcycle *(below)* was originally purchased by Charles A. Lindbergh while he was still in college. Motorcycles are enjoying a revived popularity today.

Though derived from the basic European farm wagon, no horse-drawn vehicle is more typically American, nor more historically significant than the graceful "Conestoga" covered freight wagon *(above)*. It originated in the Conestoga River Valley of the Pennsylvania-Dutch County of Lancaster. Traditionally the wagons were constructed with wide metal-tired wheels for sturdy support. Wagon accessories often included an ornamental toolbox on the side *(left)*, a feed-trough slung on the back, a tallow bucket, a jack, and an ever-handy axe. A later derivation of the Conestoga wagon was the western prairie schooner.

The 1892 horse-drawn tank wagon *(above)* is one of more than six thousand originally used by Standard Oil Company to deliver kerosene for heating and lighting to the farmers in the area between Chicago and Detroit. Early farm tractors and stationary engines also ran on kerosene. As automobiles became more numerous after 1910, many of these wagons were diverted to hauling gasoline and oil to accommodate the new mode of transportation. Horse-drawn wagons, even at this late date, were used instead of motor trucks because they could more easily negotiate the muddy midwestern roadways.

The first commercial truck-trailer *(below)* was produced in 1914 for a 1911 Model T Ford by the Fruehauf Trailer Company, Detroit, Michigan, for use by the Sibley Lumber Company. August C. Fruehauf and Otto Neumann fashioned the trailer in a blacksmith shop on Gratiot Avenue. This was the beginning of the great tractor-trailer industry which Americans depend upon for freight transportation.

One-Horse Shay, circa 1870.

Until World War I, Americans relied largely on horse-drawn vehicles for transportation. Any travel, other than local, was something of an adventure. Only the wealthy could afford a comfortable, sprung carriage.

Although of European origin, the one-horse, two-wheeled chaise (corrupted to shay) was popular in America because of its low cost, convenience, and adaptability to poor roads. The shay *(left, top)*, suspended by leather through braces on a wooden

Governor's Barouche, 1870.

General Lafayette's Phaeton, circa 1820.

Phaeton Baby Carriage, circa 1885.

Four-Wheel Buggy, 1830.

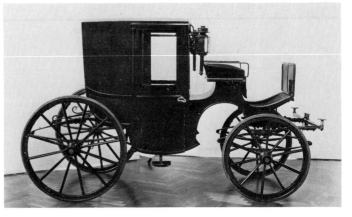

Brougham, 1901–1909.

cantilever spring, was built by Elmer P. Sargent in Merrimac, Massachusetts, for Dr. G. G. Clement of nearby Haverhill.

The Phaeton was a very graceful, light, personal carriage which usually had side panels carved to resemble the shape of a scalloped seashell. It differed from the chaise in that the front wheels prevented the jogging motion of the horse from being transmitted through the shafts to the passenger. The Marquis de Lafayette's personal Phaeton *(far left)* is unique in its three-wheel design. It was brought from France in 1824 on the occasion of his second visit to America. While recuperating from an illness in the Verplanck homestead at Brinckerhoff, New York, he rode daily in the vehicle.

The four-wheeled buggy has long been used by both farmers and townsmen for personal transportation. The light buggy with its high, spindly wheels and end-bar suspension on two transverse, full elliptical steel springs *(far left)*, was built by William C. Fauber in Lebanon, Pennsylvania.

Comfort and elegance are exemplified by the barouche, favorite of wealthy urbanites. The graceful carriage *(near left, top)*, called "The Governor's Coach," was built at a cost of ten thousand dollars by the E. M. Miller Company of Quincy, Illinois, and was used in Nevada for affairs of state. Many celebrities, including Theodore Roosevelt, rode in this carriage. Elegant coachwork is enhanced by the silver door handles and mountings recalling the fabulous bonanza days of early Nevada history.

An opulent baby carriage is a detailed, miniaturized form of the "George IV Phaeton," a vehicle favored by that English monarch.

England's Lord Henry Brougham had a two-passenger, enclosed vehicle built to his specifications so that he could readily enter through a tall door in its drop-center body. This Brougham *(near left, bottom)* was purchased during the administration of President Theodore Roosevelt, and was used by him and succeeding Presidents on official occasions until its retirement in 1928.

In general, the basic design of a horse-drawn carriage was not readily adapted to automotive power. One rare exception is this Roper steam carriage *(below)*, oldest existing and fully operative car in America. It was built in 1863 by Sylvester H. Roper of Roxbury, Massachusetts, and exhibited at country fairs in New England and the Middle West during the 1860s and 1870s. Usually it was pitted against the best trotting horses at the fairs and always won. The car had no brakes; the operator stopped by shutting off the steam to the two-cylinder, oscillating-type engine. Steering was by rack-and-pinion, a design being used in automobiles today. Between 1860 and 1896, Roper built ten steam-powered vehicles including several steam motorcycles.

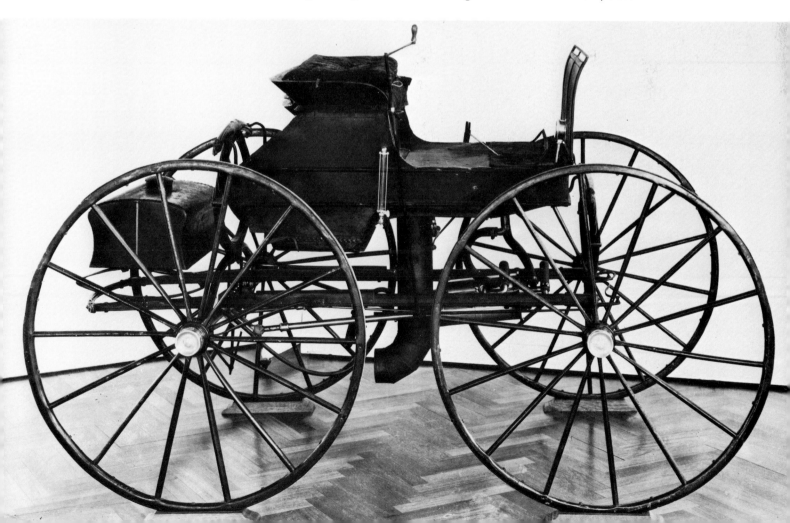

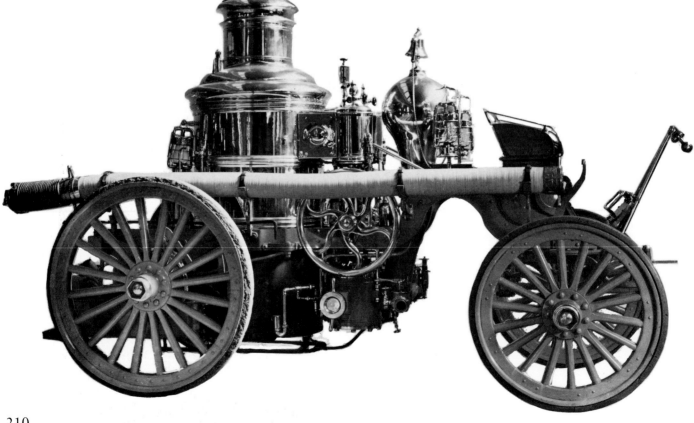

The horse-drawn fire engine weathervane *(above)* was made by Cushing & White, Waltham, Massachusetts, and dates circa 1875–1900. It is one of many transportation-related vanes in the Folk Art Collection. The steam-pressured pump on this colorful piece relates it to an actual engine *(below)* originally used by the Manchester, New Hampshire, Fire Department. The vertical boiler and combustion chamber was manufactured by the Manchester Locomotive Works and patented on August 8, 1882. The engine was rebuilt in 1900 and put into service by the Detroit Fire Department. The early, leather fireman's hat *(left),* the brass-trimmed fire belts *(right),* and the fire hat emblem *(center, bottom)* were standard equipment for early fire-fighters.

The hand-drawn fire engine *(above)* was manufactured by L. Button & Son at Waterford, New York, in 1873. Volunteer Engine Company #2 of West Newbury, Massachusetts, converted the engine so that it could be horse-drawn. The earliest form of mobile fire fighting equipment was the fire engine *(below)* made by Gleason & Bailey at Seneca Falls, New York, circa 1850. This hand-pump, hand-drawn engine greatly increased fire-fighter efficiency, replacing the "bucket brigade" with suction hoses that could operate from a nearby stream.

The birchbark canoe (above), a native to America, was adopted as a means of individual transportation by explorers and adventurers. Early commercial travel in America was by wooden sailing vessels, frequently built in New England. The clipper ships of the 1850s represented the epitome of speed in sailing. A Currier and Ives print (right) illustrates one of the shipwrights' most beautiful creations—the Flying Cloud clipper built by Donald McKay at East Boston, Massachusetts, in 1851. This 1,750-ton, 225-foot vessel still holds the unbroken record of only 89 days sailing out of New York to San Francisco around South America. The small sailboat design called the "catboat" was popular with mid-nineteenth-century sports enthusiasts and is still in limited use today. The 1860 Sprite (left) was designed and built by the Herreshoff marine architects at Bristol, Rhode Island.

Early life-saving equipment is rare. This longboat (right) with its shore equipment, circa 1870, is marked "Humane Society, Mass." and was last used in 1914 when the barkentine Beatrice was stranded on Brass Rip Pass off Nantucket, Massachusetts.

Ore ships, designed especially for use on the Great Lakes, are a vital link in the transportation of materials for the automobile industry. The motorship Henry Ford II, built in 1924 by the American Shipbuilding Company at Loraine, Ohio, is represented in the Museum by a 76-inch model (below). She and her sister ship, Benson Ford, were for many years the only large diesel-powered ore ships on the Great Lakes.

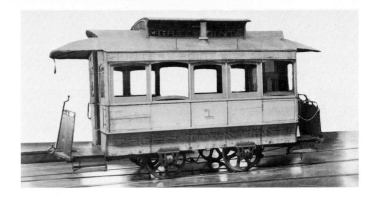

Steam-powered rail transportation had its inception in England, but attained a high degree of development in America.

One of the earliest locomotives in the collections is the *DeWitt Clinton (left, top)* built by John B. Jervis in 1831 at the West Point Foundry, New York. It was the first train to run in New York State and the third in America. The passenger coaches, built by Gould at Troy, New York, were merely conventional stagecoaches set on flanged iron wheels.

The wood-burning, "American" type locomotive *(left),* built by the Rogers Locomotive Works, Paterson, New Jersey, in 1858, saw service in the Civil War. Restored by Henry Ford and supplied with hand-painted wooden coaches, it was used in the dedication ceremonies of The Edison Institute in 1929.

Streetcars drawn on steel rails by horses provided better, smoother, and slightly faster transportation within cities than the older road coach or omnibus. This coach was built, circa 1881, by the J. M. Jones & Company of West Troy, New York, and used by the Brooklyn Railroad Company until 1897 *(top, center).*

A manpower shortage brought about by World War I inspired Charles Birney to invent the 1917 "Safety," double-end streetcar *(left),* in which one man served as both conductor and motorman. Used mostly on one-track suburban runs, the operator simply reversed the "trolley" pole, moved to the opposite end of the car, and made the return trip.

The giant six-hundred-ton steam locomotive *Allegheny (below)* was made in Ohio at the Lima Locomotive Works in 1941. It was one of the last and largest coal-burning locomotives built in the United States. Before retirement, it traveled over four hundred thousand miles hauling coal from West Virginia, Virginia, and Kentucky.

The local depot, like the general store, was once a focal point of town and village social and business life —a place where American youth could gaze in awe at the mighty "iron horse" and occasionally meet their engineer heroes. This railroad station of the Civil War period is complete with all the equipment used by a stationmaster and train crew.

Aviation was born in America in 1903 with the first manned flight by Wilbur and Orville Wright. Six years later, Louis Bleriot, pioneer French airman, made the first flight across the English Channel in his monoplane. A similar Bleriot airplane *(below)* is preserved in the Museum's collection of historic civilian aircraft which also includes two Polar and one Arctic exploration airplanes. Earliest of these is the 1926 Fokker wood-and-fabric, trimotored monoplane *(left, top)* built by Tony Fokker of Holland. Sponsored by Edsel Ford and named *Josephine Ford,* the plane was flown over the North Pole by Admiral Richard E. Byrd in 1926. Three years later, Byrd flew the 1928 all-metal Ford trimotor monoplane *(left, center)* over the South Pole. The Ford trimotor, one of the greatest of all airplanes, is still in commercial use between the Lake Erie islands. It was the first all-metal, multipassenger, multiengine transport airplane; first to make regular, scheduled commercial flights; first to be guided by radio beacon; first to have flight stewards; and first to have "in flight" motion picture shows. The 1929 Lockheed "Vega" *(left, bottom)* is the earliest of its kind extant. Because of its streamlined design, introduced in 1927, and lightweight "monocoque" plywood construction, the "Vega" could attain greater speed than its contemporary transport airplanes. This particular "Vega" was used in 1931 by Arctic explorer Donald MacMillan for mapping Arctic Circle areas and, earlier, as a factory

demonstrator, was flown by many aviation "greats" such as Billy Mitchell, Wiley Post, Amelia Earhart, Henry Brown, and Charles A. Lindbergh. The world's first practical helicopter, the Vought-Sikorsky VS-300 *(above)*, established a world's endurance record on September 14, 1939, by staying aloft for 1 hour and 33 minutes. It was flown to the Henry Ford Museum by its designer, Igor Sikorsky, and is now suspended from the ceiling of the huge Mechanical Arts Hall.

1912 Milk Wagon

The horse-drawn milk wa-
gon was one of the most familiar sights in American towns
until replaced by the modern
dairy truck. Bringing bottled
milk at dawn from door to
door, it was the successor to
the hand cart and wagon of
earlier generations of milkmen
who measured out milk from

cans into the
containers

This wagon
ample of its type,
decorated about 1
lyn, New York
Schnabel, wagonm
rer Schnell, pain
by dairyman, Will
Englewood, N

218

IV. Special Exhibitions

Through the presentation of special exhibitions, the Henry Ford Museum fulfills its educational role. Many times each year, objects for an in-depth study of a specific collection are gathered from both the Village and Museum and placed on view in the special exhibition galleries. Traveling shows such as the photographic presentation, "The Family of Man" sponsored by the Museum of Modern Art in New York City, and loan exhibitions like the Henry Ford Museum's thousand-item exhibit, "Midwest Collectors' Choice," are part of the special exhibitions program. The annual "Sports Car Show" (below) is presented in an effort to bring to the public a visual demonstration of the more significant steps in the development of our present-day automobile. A dramatic vehicle such as the Bugatti Royale (above) never fails to impress, for it was designed to be of such size and elegance that it would shame every other pretentious classic car. "The Gwinn Dairy Exhibition" (left), an astonishing collection of some fifteen hundred objects, books, and documents related to the dairy industry history, celebrates a gift of David M. Gwinn to the agricultural collection begun by Henry Ford.

Each year the Museum sponsors the Midwest Antiques Forum. Focusing on a central theme, *"Collecting Americana,"* world-renowned experts in specific fields of the decorative arts lecture to participants who travel from all parts of the country to attend these informative and popular sessions. A special exhibition relating to the overall theme of the Forum provides a three-dimensional extension of the illustrated lectures. In recent years, "The Craftsmanship of Quality" and "Selected Treasures of the Henry Ford Museum" brought into sharp focus the scope and depth of the Museum's decorative arts collections. The radio *(right)* was featured in an important special presentation, "Talking Box to Telstar," which commemorated the fiftieth anniversary of the broadcasting industry.

"Talking Box to Telstar"

Queen Anne display in "A Decade and a Half of Collecting" Exhibition.

"The Craftsmanship of Quality"

The creation of Christmas wreaths, cedar and holly roping, and other traditional decorations is a colorful demonstration given by Museum craftsmen during the holiday season. A woodcarver *(left)* creates toys in the special exhibition, "Crafts at Christmas." A group of room settings in the "Home for Christmas" show *(below)* illustrates how our ancestors celebrated one of their most treasured holidays.

The Clara B. Ford Garden Forum, a three-day annual event at the Henry Ford Museum, is always accompanied by a special exhibition *(right).* In addition to a full program of illustrated morning and evening lectures, afternoon discussion sessions, and nature walks, participants enjoy the opportunity of conversing with experts and other garden enthusiasts.

The American Drama Festival, inaugurated in the summer of 1964 at the Henry Ford Museum, presents the Greenfield Village Players—one of the few repertory companies devoted exclusively to the production of early dramas by American playwrights. In addition, it provides facilities for education and instruction in the arts of the theater.

V. American Drama Festival

The American Drama Festival has increased its repertoire from two plays over a six-week period to four plays during a ten-week summer season. Additional performances are given at Christmas and Easter. At other times during the year, the Theater Arts Department presents varied programs of musical concerts, dance recitals, nineteenth-century readings, and early motion pictures. The museum-sponsored Theater Arts Apprentice Program furthers the principle of encouraging talented youth begun by Mr. and Mrs. Henry Ford in their lifetimes. Some of the early plays presented are *Shenandoah,* first performed in 1889; *Rip Van Winkle,* originally produced in 1865; *The Henrietta,* first performed on September 26, 1887; and *Under the Gaslight (below),* which opened on August 12, 1867. During intermission, while the audience sips lemonade under the stars in the torchlit courtyard *(left),* they are serenaded by the actors who then lead them back into the theater for the second half of the performance.

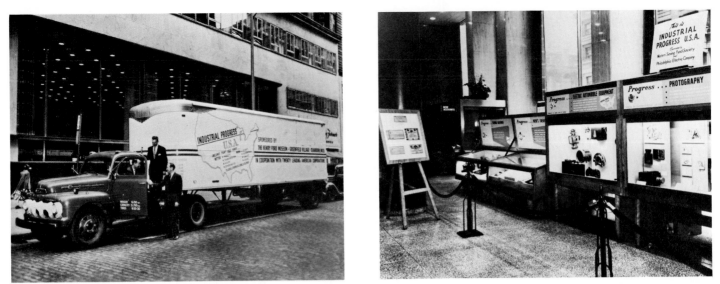

"Industrial Progress, U.S.A.," a traveling exhibit which visited cities across the United States from 1952 through 1955.

"Schoolroom Progress, U.S.A.," a traveling display contrasting early American schools with the latest equipment of the 1950s.

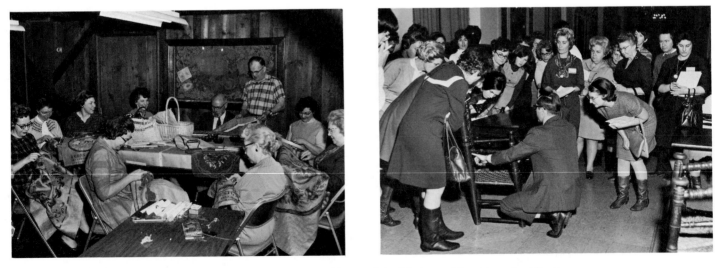

Adult Education classes: Rug Hooking and the History of American Furniture.

VI. Educational Activities

The Adult Education Division provides an opportunity to become better acquainted with early American artifacts and culture. Collections at the Museum and Village serve as teaching aids in a series of enrichment courses taught by members of the Museum's professional staff. Subjects offered are American furniture, clocks, glass, metals, automobiles, the rifle, and decorating with antiques.

Instruction in various early American crafts include glassblowing, dried flower arranging, spinning, weaving, pottery-making, metalworking, and chair-caning.

In conjunction with the University of Michigan, the Museum offers a two-year graduate program leading to a Master of Museum Practice degree. A joint effort with the Adult Education Division of Wayne State University and the Michigan State University coordinates graduate courses with workshops for teachers. The Division also works with individual professors at a number of Michigan colleges to arrange short sessions utilizing the Museum and Village in a variety of academic fields. The Adult Education Division, with other facilities, is housed in the Education Building. On the second floor of this structure is *Lovett Hall (below),* a grand ballroom named for Benjamin B. Lovett, the dancing master Mr. Ford brought from Massachusetts to teach early American dancing.

The Library of the Henry Ford Museum is one of the great research centers for scholars of American history. Over two hundred thousand books, pamphlets, periodicals, and ephemeral items in the reference section are devoted to all phases of Americana. The rare book and manuscript collections contain treasures which offer original background and source material relating to the United States from its Colonial days to the present. Pilgrim settlers probably brought with them copies of a 1611 translated Bible now known as the King James Version *(above)*. The self-portrait by John Watson (1685–1768) *(near right),* the watercolor "Profile of the Carriage of George Washington" *(below, left),* Washington's bookplate *(below, right),* and the 1779 State of Massachusetts Bay Lottery Certificate *(far right, bottom),* along with holograph letters and important historic documents relating to early political and military leaders, vividly portray the American story. An integral part of the Library is the map collection. A sixteenth-century map by Sebastian Munster *(far right, top)* was the first to depict the American continent. Other maps illustrate sections of the country, states, and plans of cities and forts.

Profile of the Carriage of George Washington

EXITUS ACTA PROBAT

George Washington

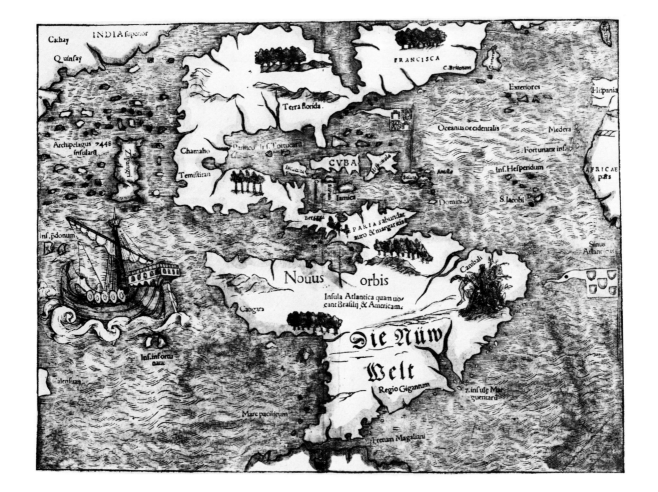

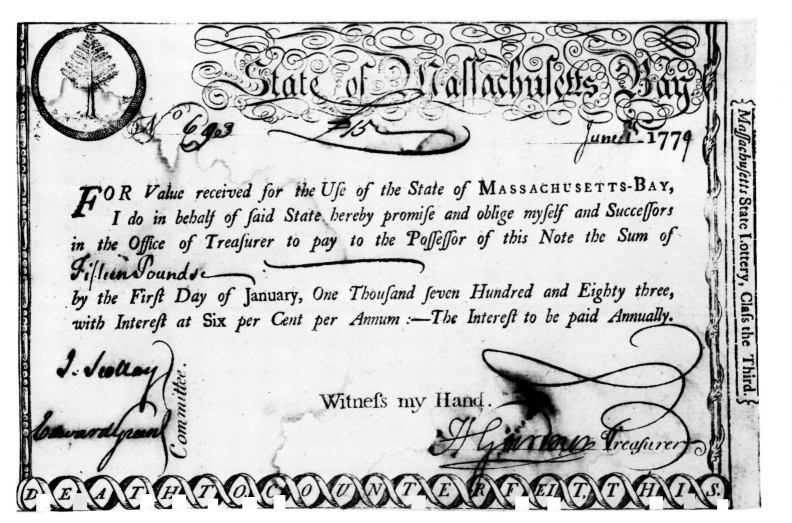

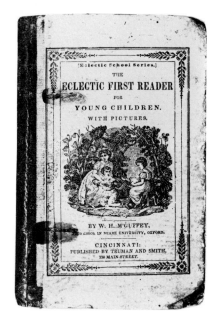

The *Bloody Massacre* (left), an event which took place in Boston, Massachusetts, on March 5, 1770, and which sparked the American Revolution, was engraved, printed, and sold by Paul Revere. The Museum's copy is one of two known which were hand-colored and signed by Christian Remich. Military engagements were always a popular subject. The Currier and Ives print, published in 1862 (right, bottom), shows the *Battle of Fredericksburg*, Virginia, in December 1862 during the Civil War.

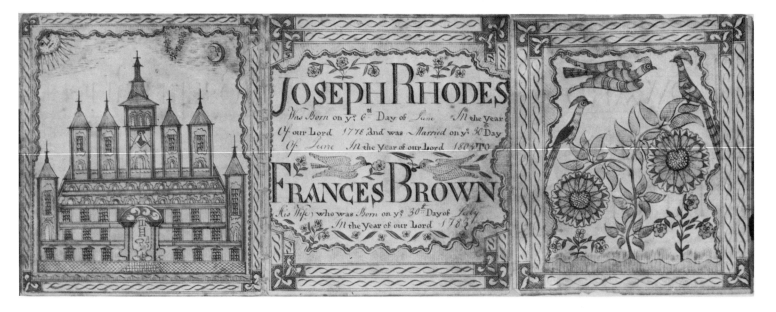

colorful Seminole leader, is shown before Indian tents proudly displaying his rifle in an 1842 lithograph published by Daniel Rice and James G. Clark of Philadelphia, Pennsylvania. It was drawn, printed, and colored at J. T. Bowen's Lithographic Establishment. The painted fraktur by John Barnard (far left, bottom) is probably from Ohio, circa 1803, and represents a relatively large group of such pieces executed by the artist. The libraries contained within original buildings in nearby Greenfield Village are, for the most part, associated with the famous owners such as Thomas Alva Edison's books, manuscripts, and papers in the Menlo Park buildings, the personal books in the Wright brothers' home, and the Luther Burbank office collection. The library in the Joseph Pearson Secretary House matches an original inventory of the house taken in 1823. One of the most treasured groups of books in the Museum Library is a collection of all editions of McGuffey Readers, assembled by Mr. and Mrs. Henry Ford in 1914. This was their first collecting effort and the one which ultimately led to their founding The Edison Institute.

Represented in the print collection are all of the outstanding American printmakers including Peter Pelham, Paul Revere, Nathaniel Hurd, Amos Doolittle, Currier and Ives, Louis Prang, and the Kelloggs. Osceola, a

CURRIER & IVES.   Entered according to act of Congress in the year 1862, by Currier & Ives, in the Clerks Office of the District Court of the United States, for the Southern District of New York   152 NASSAU ST NEW

BATTLE OF FREDERICKSBURG, V.ª DEC. 13TH 1862.

This battle shows with what undaunted courage, the Lion-hearted Army of the Potomac always meets its foes... After forcing the passage of the Rappahannock on the 11th in the face of a murderous fire from concealed Rebels, and taking possession of Fredericksburg on the 12th, on the morning of the 13th the Army rushed with desperate valor on the intrenchments of the enemy, and thousands of its dead and dying, tell of the fearful strife which raged till night put an end to the carnage. Though driven back by an intrenched and hidden foe, the Soldiers of the North are still as ready to meet the Traitors of the South, as in their days of proudest victory.

Left: Henry Ford's personal holdings of capital stock in the Ford Motor Company in 1903 were 255 shares.

VIII. Ford Archives

The Ford Archives, presented to The Edison Institute in 1964, are housed in the Henry Ford Museum. They are the largest collection of records known that relate to a single individual, his family, his broad personal interests, his philanthropic achievements, and the worldwide business he founded. Fourteen million documents, books, and manuscripts and some four hundred fifty thousand original photographic negatives form this rich, significant research collection that extends virtually to the present day. It is also the most comprehensive non-governmental resource covering American personalities and events of the first half of the twentieth century. These unique, comparatively unpublished materials are readily available to qualified scholars and historians.

On the second floor of the Museum, a permanent exhibition, entitled "Henry Ford, A Personal History," is dedicated to the memory of the man whose creative influence reshaped today's world. The elements of his daily life, his first homemade tools, and the many honors and gifts that later came to him in recognition of his accomplishments have all been carefully selected and arranged to tell the success story of Henry Ford's rise from a Dearborn farm boy to a genius of world renown.

Left: Henry Ford and the Quadricycle, his first gasoline-powered vehicle, on the streets of Detroit, Michigan, in October, 1896.

Below: Ford developed his first gasoline engine on the kitchen sink of his home at 58 Bagley Avenue, Detroit, Michigan. Mrs. Ford kept the engine running by supplying it with gasoline from a medicine dropper.

On April 1, 1913, Henry Ford began using his newly developed moving assembly line at the Highland Park, Michigan, plant. Through the installation of such innovative concepts as the body drop *(below)*, production was increased from seventy-five thousand to three hundred thousand cars a year.

The Ford Model T was first produced in 1908. In May of 1927, the fifteen millionth and last of this model *(left)* came off the assembly line.

Ford's oak-paneled Highland Park office was the center of the Ford industry. The Museum exhibit *(bottom)* is a full-scale installation using the original paneling and office furniture.

Bottom: Nothing better illustrates the diversity of Henry Ford's mind than his many friends and acquaintances from all walks of life. He was the friend-in-common who united three seemingly different individuals—the tire manufacturer Harvey Firestone, Sr., the inventor Thomas Alva Edison, and the naturalist John Burroughs. These men, calling themselves the "Four Vagabonds," traveled from the Florida Everglades to Michigan's Upper Peninsula searching for unspoiled forest areas where they could enjoy outdoor life. In 1921, Warren G. Harding, President of the United States, joined the group for a rustic banquet and dined with them at the large folding table that is now featured in the Personal History display.

Center: The opening of the 1939 New York World's Fair was attended by dignitaries from the world over. Participating in the dedication ceremonies were Grover Whalen, Henry Ford II, Edsel Ford, Henry Ford, Alfred E. Smith, and Fiorello La Guardia.

Above: Henry Ford's three grandsons, Benson, Henry Ford II, and William Clay, have followed the footsteps of their grandfather and their father, Edsel Ford, in the preservation of America's heritage. Serving for many years as members of the Board of Trustees, with William Clay as Chairman, they are continuing to further the development of The Edison Institute.

Index

Index

Page numbers in *italics* indicate an illustration.

243